Barb
Thank you for all you
support you give to
Students
Alana

BEVERLEY

Beverley: The Stories and Artwork of an Exceptional School

Collected and edited by Robert Bickford

Published by Life Rattle Press, Toronto, Canada
Copyright 2013 by the contributing authors.

Library and Archives Canada Cataloguing in Publication

Beverley: The stories and artwork of an exceptional school / collected and edited by Robert Bickford.

(New writers series ; 1200-5266)
ISBN 978-1-927023-59-4 (pbk.)
1. Beverley School (Toronto, Ont.)--Biography.
2. Students with disabilities--Ontario--Toronto.
3. Special education--Ontario--Toronto.
I. Bickford, Robert, 1982-, editor of compilation
II. Series: Life Rattle new writers series

LC3984.3.T67B48 2013   371.909713'541   C2013-907473-2

Edited: Robert Bickford and Laurie Kallis
Proofread: Stephanie Cheung, John Dunford
Photography: Robert Bickford, Michael Pivar
Cover Artwork: Alexander Sam
Typeset: Laurie Kallis

THE STORIES AND ARTWORK OF AN EXCEPTIONAL SCHOOL

BEVERLEY

Collected by Robert Bickford

Life Rattle Press   Toronto, Canada

CONTENTS

I Am The Child
AUTHOR UNKNOWN. 1

Resiliency
BY AFSHAN ALI 4

Noel Hats
BY ALANA GROSSMAN 7

A Mini-Staycation
BY AMANDA WILLIAMS 13

Paul
BY ANGELE CORRIVEAU 18

Sandrine
BY ANGELE CORRIVEAU 19

Gaining Perspective
BY ANNE POLLETT 21

Toy Doctor:
Playing and Learning at Sunny View PS
BY ANNIE APPLEBY 27

Through Your Brother's Eyes
    BY BECKY QUINLAN 31

Lessons from Maddie
    BY CHERYL FORD 35

Michael
    BY CHRISTINE MARTENS 41

Robert
    BY CHRISTINE MARTENS 43

Hard to Soft
    BY DAVE ASQUINI 45

Camp Couchiching
    BY DAVID CAMPOS 49

Saul
    BY DAVID ROLFE. 53

Blessed
    BY DENNIS THOMSON 55

Let me Introduce You To Madison
    BY DOUG FORD 57

Lessons
    BY ELLEN SCHWARTZ 61

Dancing Our Way to Integration
    BY FRANCES BERMAN 75

Once Upon a Niece
    BY HEIDI MITCHELL 79

Jake's Story: 1
    BY JAKE LIGHTFOOT 85

Jake's Story: 2
    BY JAKE LIGHTFOOT 89

The Lion Sleeps Tonight
    BY JAMES CONNOR 93

Conrad
    BY JAN GRIFFITHS. 99

Asma
    BY JANET LEWIS. 105

Maddie
    BY JANET LEWIS. 107

Jake and Me
    BY JANINE DENNEY-LIGHTFOOT 109

Thoughts From an Intervenor
    BY JENNIFER MAYR. 113

Neil
    BY JENNIFER ABELL 115

Autism in the Azores
    BY JENNIFER THOMPSON FERREIRA 119

Being a Family
    BY JORDAN CLELAND 129

Tricked
    BY JULIE GRANT 139

More Than Things
    BY KEITHA HALSTEAD AND ASMA MEDINA 141

To The Point
    BY LAURA JOHNSTON 143

Hello, My Name is Lexie
    BY LEXIE FERREIRA 147

the Beamer
    BY LYDIA SAI-CHEW 151

Lessons from the Beamer
    BY LYDIA SAI-CHEW 155

Johnnie's Poem
    BY MADELEINE STANDISH 159

Conchi's Bus
    BY MARIA GUERRA DECASTRO 161

My Greatest Teacher
    BY MICHAEL-JAMES PALAZZO 165

Who We Are
    BY NICKI CAMPBELL 169

Beverley Kids Will Teach You
    BY REBECCA ANSLEY 175

Room 110
    BY ROBERT BICKFORD 177

Yes and No
    BY ROBERT BICKFORD 185

Beverley School
    BY SABRINA MOREY 189

Coming of Age
    BY SPENCER STANDISH 193

Thank You for Your Children
    BY STACIE CARROLL 197

Blowing Bubbles
    BY STELLA KYRIACOU 200

Swimming
    BY STELLA KYRIACOU 201

My Sister Tenny
    BY STEPHANIE QUANCE. 203

The Story of Zhela Lerwob
    BY STEPHEN SUEN 207

Once Upon A Time
    BY SUZANNE HEARN. 211

Mothers of Beverley
    BY TRACY PARSONS. 215

Oh, Beverley
    BY ZOFIA CZERNIAWSKA 218

Beverley School Student Quilt Project

I AM THE CHILD

AUTHOR UNKNOWN

Contributed to the Our-Kids e-mail group by Peter Jones, Oct 17, 1995. This story is transcribed from a memorial letter and read aloud by the parents of a Beverley student, Timothy, who passed away two years ago.

I am the child who cannot talk.

You often pity me. I see it in your eyes. You wonder how much I am aware of. I see that as well. I am aware of much...whether you are happy or sad or fearful, patient or impatient, full of love and desire, or if you are just doing your duty by me. I marvel at your frustration, knowing mine to be far greater, for I cannot express myself or my needs as you do. You cannot conceive my isolation, so complete it is at times.

I do not gift you with clever conversation or cute remarks to be laughed over and repeated. I do not give you answers to your everyday questions, responses over my well being, or share my needs or comments about the world around me. I do not give you rewards as defined by the world's standards or great strides in development that you can credit yourself. I do not give you understanding as you know it.

What I give you is so much more valuable. I give you instead opportunities. Opportunities to discover the depth of your character, not mine; the depth of your love, your commitment, your patience, your abilities; the opportunity to explore your spirit more deeply than you imagined possible. I drive you further than you would ever go on your own, working harder, seeking answers to your many questions with no answers. I am the child who cannot talk.

I am the child who cannot walk.

The world seems to pass me by. You see the longing in my eyes to get out of this chair, to run and play like other children. There is much you take for granted. I want the toys on the shelf, I need to go to the bathroom, oh I've dropped my fork again. I am dependant on you in these ways.

My gift to you is to make you more aware of your great fortune, your healthy back and legs, your ability to do for yourself. Sometimes people appear not to notice me; I always notice them. I feel not so much envy as desire, desire to stand upright, to put one foot in front of the other, to be independent. I give you awareness. I am the child who cannot walk.

I am the child who is mentally impaired.

I don't learn easily, if you judge me by the world's measuring stick. What I do know is infinite joy in simple things. I am not burdened as you are with the strifes and conflicts of a more complicated life.

My gift to you is to grant you the freedom to enjoy things as a child, to teach you how much your arms around me mean, to give you love. I give you the gift of simplicity. I am the child who is mentally impaired.

I am the disabled child.

I am your teacher. if you allow me, I will teach you what is really important in life. I will give you and teach you unconditional love. I gift you with my innocent trust, my dependency upon you. I teach you about how precious this life is and about not taking things for granted. I teach you about forgetting your own needs and desires and dreams. I teach you giving. Most of all I teach you hope and faith. I am the disabled child.

Beverley CD Cover Project

RESILIENCY

BY AFSHAN ALI

Have you ever noticed how every now and then you will see a tree, flower or plant, sprout in the most unlikely places? They manage to squeeze through concrete, rock and brick to flourish into beautiful living things despite their unfertile environments. Although the resources needed to grow are sparse, these living things do what comes naturally to them—they blossom and grow.

Such is the case with human beings—especially children. We arrive in this world without the ability to choose our environments. We all face adversity in different forms and shapes. However, our natural instinct to survive and flourish carries us through the hardest times, allowing us to beat the odds and overcome whatever challenges we face. This is the foundation of my philosophy of education: fostering and honing this natural instinct that we're born with—resiliency.

As a Master of Teaching candidate at the Ontario Institute for Studies in Education, my particular area of research involves the investigation of pedagogy and practices aimed at fostering resiliency in students with Autism Spectrum Disorder. During my time in the program I was granted the opportunity to complete a practicum at Beverley School. I worked alongside the most brilliant and dedicated educators in special education, and I was fortunate enough to spend four wonderful weeks with seven exceptional children who taught me the true meaning of resiliency.

I would like to share some of the lessons that my students at Beverley School taught me.

Resiliency means taking risks, like putting your fingers into cold, gooey paint, and experimenting with weird objects like cotton balls, flower petals and even glitter to create wonderful pieces of art—even when it feels scary and uncomfortable.

Resiliency means having the courage to throw the ball to one of your classmates, even if they might not throw the ball back.

Resiliency means enduring through the difficult moments. Whether it's sitting through a noisy Friday afternoon music session, crossing that unfamiliar street on an afternoon walk or jumping into the water of the swimming pool.

Resiliency means knowing and taking pleasure in each and every success.

Most importantly, resiliency means having a smile on your face and enjoying every moment of every day.

Beverley Summer School Project

NOEL HATS

BY ALANA GROSSMAN

I am sitting in my office at seven-thirty on a March morning, chatting away, when John's father walks in. He's a tall man with salt and pepper hair, almost like a forties movies star.

John was a student here, who died two years ago. His father, though reducing the number of trips, still visits many times during the year but especially on John's birthday.

His step is lighter this year and his tears are less frequent.

We hug. He's a very affectionate man and likes to hug. Even his hug feels lighter, less full of grief and pain. I always enjoy his hugs; they have meaning and depth. Different parents hug me for different reasons and it is a mystery trying to find out what the emotion or the need is. With John's dad, that is just who he is. He conveys meaning and I enjoy hugging him; it is affirming.

John's father pulls out eleven frog hats or should I say "Noel" hats. John always carried around a plush toy frog that we called Noel; it was even buried with John. The hats that John's father pulls out remind us all of John's Noel. Whenever I see a frog, I think of John. Unfortunately, I mostly see toads when I'm gardening and have not made the association, but I might in the future.

I put on the Noel hat and pay homage to John.

I was raised in a family where there was a sense of social justice, and caring and strong female role models.

My grandmother Rose used to go to the train station looking for new immigrants who had survived the Second World War and would bring them back to the house. That is how Yossi the fiddler ended up living in the attic for two years. My grandfather often came home and found a stranger sitting at the head of the table.

My mother, Anne, was a courageous woman who sold newspapers at the corner of Bay and Wellington after my father died, leaving her a widow with three young children. Gary Lautens wrote an article about her in *The Toronto Star* entitled "A Lady's Backbone is Made of Steel not China."

In my thirty-six-year career in special education as an educator and an administrator, I have been privileged to learn so much from students and their families, from around the world.

In New Zealand, it was a great honour to be part of a Maori welcoming ceremony and to be greeted into my place of employment by the elder of the marae, while his wife chanted. As a Maori welcome, I rubbed noses with about sixty people. Now that is community.

As a vice principal in a Section school, which is a partnership between school boards and ministry agencies for youth in treatment, detention and hospitalization facilities, I worked with the hardest-to-serve students and their families. This experience challenged the way in which I had previously viewed how the social structures of our society respond to young people who have mental health issues and/or break the law.

During a Sub-Saharan African safari, I visited Kenya and travelled down the Mali River to Timbuktu. On this river boat ride, I stayed beside a family of seven who shared one bed! From there, I went on to visit India, a country that is beautiful in every way.

On my return, I started to work for the Women's Federation as a collective bargaining representative. My four-year stint included a month-long strike. I have experienced working in education during the consecutive rule of all three major political parties. In the ten years that I worked as a low incidence consultant, my job constantly changed, as the definition, philosophy and face of special education were constantly changing.

As principal of Beverley School, I have come to learn how culture and ritual and celebration impact everyday learning of children with developmental disabilities and physical disabilities.

Everyday, I learn about strength, perseverance and the true meaning of celebration. At Beverley we do not have EQAO scores to compare ourselves to other schools in our system or in the world. We have a measurement of the students' quality of life.

Every time a student with a developmental disability takes a new step, speaks a new word or is able to achieve a skill not learned before, it is a testimony—first to the student, secondly to the staff. At Beverley, we cherish and gather around these moments and celebrate the student's accomplishments.

Jacob Schwartz's bar mitzvah is one of those moments, not only being a part of the joy of the celebration but also being a part of the family's journey in seeing Jacob become a "bar mitzvah boucher." The event is all about community and how, as an adult, you take part in your tribe.

The rabbi embraced Jacob into the Jewish community and talked about how his life has affected so many people in so many ways. In every religion, there is a quest towards the one, and the light to guide into spiritual enlightenment comes from many sources. It is possible that Jacob's purpose is to help many people find in their hearts that light, through the work that his parents and community have begun.

The celebration started at Beverley School. We hoisted Jacob in a mechanical lift, the same one used to transfer him from his wheelchair each day, and all the staff and students held hands and danced the hora. He had a wonderful smile on his face until we threw candies at him in the age-old tradition to wish him a sweet and healthy life. His face had the look "are these people nuts!" The same look of horror was on his face as the congregation threw the same candies at him the next day.

It is the rituals that define a people but it is love that defines who you are and who you become. His parents have given a voice to Jacob's heart and found a wider purpose for his life. They shared this with many people from Jacob's life and community. Each of the guests in the room participated in lighting one of the thirteen candles to celebrate his birthday.

On the matchbooks was a print of Jacob's hand and a thank you to everyone who helps light up his life. I am very proud that Beverley School plays a crucial part in Jacob's life and community, but Jacob and his family are very significant in teaching us lessons about life, about strength, and most of all about community and acceptance.

The Noel frog hats, the ones that John's dad dropped off on his birthday, in a playful way, honour John's contribution to the school and to each of our lives. There is always someone or something to remind me of our special students, not in a sad way, but in a way that makes me just smile.

That is how I feel as I twirl around in my office wearing a Noel frog hat. I smile, grateful that so many people have given me hugs that are imprinted on my body and soul forever.

Room 117 collaboration

Aman

A MINI-STAYCATION

BY AMANDA WILLIAMS

In our family, we don't go on vacations much as a group. We worry, perhaps more than we should, that our son Nathan—who has autism, a developmental delay and is non-verbal—won't be able to cope with the different surroundings and that he will become extremely anxious, which will ultimately lead to intense, prolonged meltdowns and nobody getting any sleep. Just what everybody wants while on vacation.

So, our strategy is to avoid going away on vacation, for now, and do mini-staycations. We try and take advantage of our local parks and attractions like the zoo or the science centre, knowing if Nathan is not able to tolerate the excursion, it's a short drive or walk home even in the face of a large meltdown. It's funny, though. As a parent of a child with special needs, I spend so much time thinking about what to do with Nathan when "trouble" arises, that I neglect to think about how to deal with people around us and their reactions.

Last summer, my husband, Darren, took a couple of days off work and we planned a couple of outings with Nathan and his younger brother Jack.

One day we decide to pack a lunch and take the kids to a local splash pad, which Nathan has been to before and really enjoyed. Darren and I chose this particular splash pad because it isn't as busy and crowded as others in our neighbourhood, automatically increasing the odds that this will be a pleasant experience for all of us.

Now, getting Nathan dressed requires a great deal of patience, time and physical exertion, often to the point where during the summer months, you need to take a shower after he's ready to go. Bearing that in mind on this particularly hot day, Darren and I opt to dress Nathan at the park, our thought being that once he sees the splash pad, he might be a bit more cooperative and not kick up a stink about getting undressed and into his swim trunks. We are eager to start the day. Perhaps a little too eager.

We get to the splash pad and there's no water. We're too early. They haven't turned on the sprinklers yet. Okay, we can handle this. We're at a park.

We decide to wait until the water comes on before we change Nathan into his swim trunks and head towards the play equipment. I put Jack in a bucket swing and give him a push. Nathan starts jumping up and down and squealing. He likes to watch Jack and other kids on the swings but doesn't like swinging himself. Only problem is, he has a tendency to get too close to the swings. We hold our arms in front of him to try and keep him back. He gets upset and turns away.

The sand catches his attention. That can be tricky too. Darren and I watch him like hawks because Nathan has the unpopular habit of throwing and kicking the sand.

Finally, the sprinklers come on! The laughter from the other kids gets Nathan's attention and once he sees the water, he's off. Darren runs to catch up with him, stopping only once to grab the bag with Nathan's swim trunks. I take Jack and find a place for us to set up the blanket for our picnic. I settle Jack on the blanket with some toys. I look up to see Darren, who is now completely drenched, chasing Nathan to try and get his clothes off and get his trunks on. Nathan's ear-piercing squeals tell me he's been caught and is getting changed.

Pieces of clothing are scattered across the grass. Darren comes back to the blanket to get a towel and dry off. Nathan is laughing and is watching a toddler run around in front of him. He really enjoys watching other kids move. I quickly scan the splash pad. There are only four kids including Nathan. So far, so good.

I keep watch while Darren dries off beside Jack. I decide to pick up Nathan's clothes and put them in our bag. I look up to check on Nathan only to see him push to the ground the little toddler who had stopped running and stood in front of Nathan. The push, although very inappropriate, was Nathan's way of saying, "Don't stop, keep going." The little boy is crying. I drop the clothes and run. At the same time, I hear and see the mother of the little boy pick up her son and step in front of Nathan and scream, "NO. No pushing," while pointing her finger in his face.

I reach out to Nathan and apologize to the mother for his behaviour. Nathan turns away from me and I realize that behind us, with Jack, is Darren. He also apologizes and directs Nathan, who is now getting upset, to our blanket. I explain that Nathan has autism and a delay and cannot speak. I tell her how much he enjoys watching other kids, but hasn't yet learned how to appropriately engage and communicate with other kids. Without stopping to take a breath, I tell her that Nathan was trying to tell her son to keep running, that the push wasn't intentional.

She stares at me, speechless, totally not prepared for the words coming out of my mouth. The only thing she can say is, "I didn't realize, I didn't realize." She gazes in Nathan's direction, turns, and walks away.

Without looking at him, I'm now aware that Nathan is rocking back and forth in his stroller. I turn and head towards him. He's on the verge of tears. His mouth is turned down.

Darren's gathering our things. As I help pack the stroller, I look up and scan the splash pad for the mother and toddler. No sign of them. Like ours, their outing was over before it began.

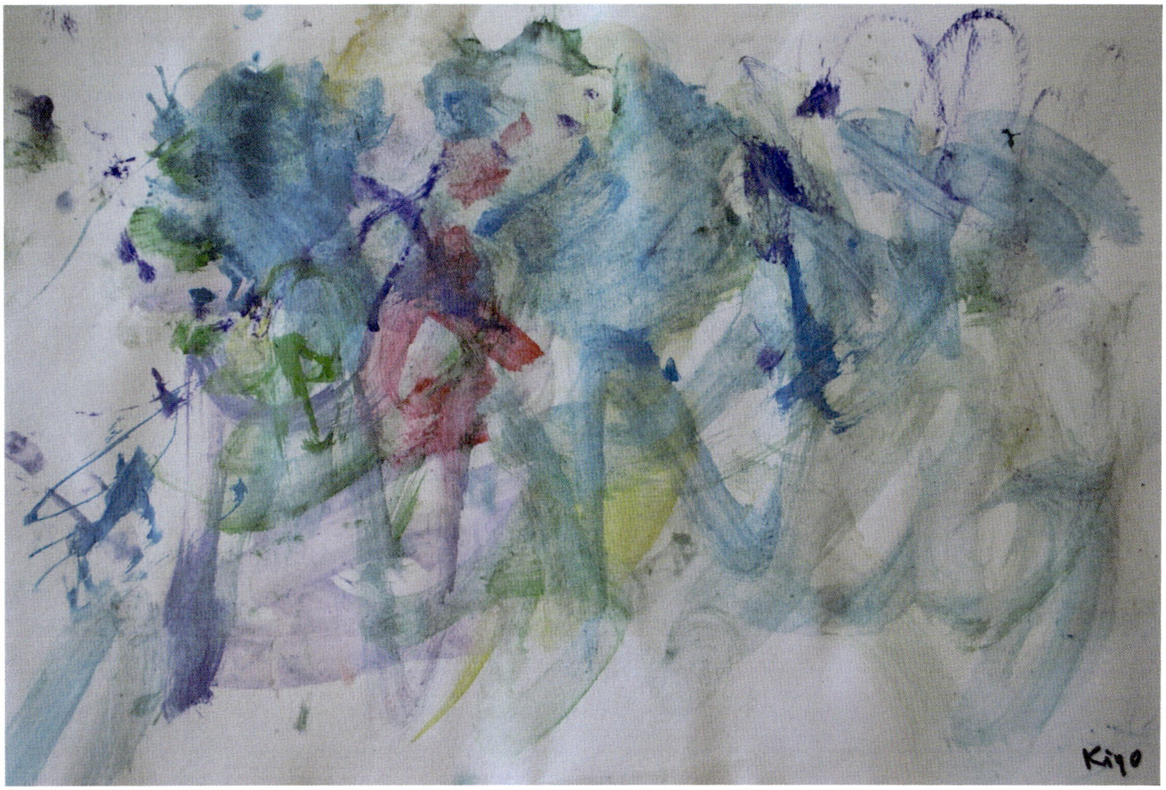
Kiyo

PAUL

BY ANGELE CORRIVEAU

We play Pictionary sometimes to encourage the students, who are all on the autism spectrum, to use their words or sign language. One of us stands at the front of the room and draws an image on the large white erase board. We draw words with clear shapes like apple, bus, ball, letter, number or fish.

One day, Dave decides to draw a guitar to see if the image would be familiar to any of the students, to see what word the image of a guitar might spark. Based on the shape, we don't know what to expect, but we look forward to hearing what our students will come up with.

Dave completes the drawing, moves away from the dry erase board, and we wait to hear an answer.

After a few seconds, Paul chimes in confidently, "A musical instrument!"

We all cheer and congratulate him.

SANDRINE

BY ANGELE CORRIVEAU

Sandrine was slapping staff members for weeks. We tried many different strategies. We redirected her attention. We asked her to make better choices. We ignored the behaviour. We used a stern voice. We used positive attention. We tried using rewards with things she enjoyed like painting her fingernails.

One afternoon, right before snack, she slaps an educational assistant. I intervene. I tell her, "You can't just slap a staff member and continue with your snack. No snack when you hit people." She sits at the table with her friends who are all eating snack. We give her a cup of water.

For ten minutes, she sips her cup of water and stares at me quietly. Near the end of snack time, I ask her, "Why do you think you didn't get your snack today?"

She raises her arm, points her finger at me and says, "Because of YOU!"

"Madonna Painting" by Victor

GAINING PERSPECTIVE

BY ANNE POLLETT

Today, I unpacked some old friends.

No, I am not a serial killer prone to love 'em, dispatch 'em and then leave 'em stowed away in a trunk somewhere. Instead, I have been quite harmless—in transition these past five years, living in my mother-in-law's renovated barn, while caring for her in these, her final years. Sadly, she passed away three weeks ago after a courageous and inspiring battle with cancer, and now we move slowly and cautiously into her farmhouse.

From the industrial shelves in the barn have come the boxes of paintings we carefully packed during our departure from Toronto. From inside pillowcases and from under layers of plastic emerge artwork by students who were more often my teachers at the Toronto District School Board, many of whom had attended Beverley School.

My romance with Beverley School began in the mid-seventies, when I was permitted to do my five-week practicum with the Metropolitan Toronto School Board. And, what a love affair it was, meeting students with musical Italian names who often lunched on chocolate (aka Nutella) sandwiches in crusty rolls. Connected by passageways to the historic George Brown building, Beverley, at that time, accommodated over one hundred and twenty students aged four to twenty-one. In the following two years, the intermediate and senior divisions were moved to the newly-built Lucy McCormick Senior School designed as a modified high school with nineteen program areas. But contained in the bricks and mortar, that seemed to inspire Beverley's renovation in the eighties, must have been the captivating spirit of creativity and innovation, which it still exudes today. Possibly it was a substance left behind as a farewell salute from the artists who moved on to Lucy, artists whose works I have unpacked these last few days.

I have always felt that I was given a rare opportunity as an art teacher, being assigned a subject that offers little possibility for failure, in a discipline that allows for the enhancement of motor skills and affords individuals an avenue to communicate their uniqueness, or, at the very least, gives them many opportunities to enjoy or reject a variety of textures, colours and smells while brandishing a selection of tools often adapted for accessibility. Although there really isn't any likelihood for error in exploring the creative arts, there is plenty of space for excellence. And for a quiet fellow named Victor, whose line drawing catches my eye now, it meant that he could be a communicating artist completely in control of his subject matter.

I can remember the astonishment in the voice of Lynne, the Community Living teacher at Lucy, when she announced at our lunch table that Victor had produced his very own transit pass, complete with his own hand-drawn portrait and carefully printed credentials, and that he had attempted to board a TTC bus, solo. For Lynne this was a clear message that he was ready and willing, in fact determined, to be trained to use the public transportation system. To me, as an art teacher, it was an obvious indication that Victor needed to be included in my advanced art classes where his work could be enhanced by artist quality brushes and paper.

At the age of fourteen, before I had an opportunity to teach him, Victor had experimented with perspective in ways he had invented on his own. He had employed unique colour combinations particularly with yellows and oranges and the complimentary blues to depict religious subjects with extraordinary detail. Particularly odd, but significant, was a painting of the Madonna cradling an obviously precocious infant Jesus, while wearing a crucifix around her neck, an anachronism no less.

In time, Victor became a member of The Art Collection, through which his paintings were exhibited extensively throughout Toronto, twice at Harbourfront, and later one of his pieces even toured China and Tai Pei where it was printed, published and awarded a gold medal. I attended an exhibition of his work in 2007, where he sold breathtaking paintings, in an advanced style that he had refined in the years since I had last seen him. I could describe Victor in terms of his syndrome and the occupations beyond his grasp, but really, what is significant is that after all those years, he was still an artist, independent and true to his craft.

Today, as I reflect on my working years in Toronto, my chosen subject area and the unique group of students I had the chance to work with, I feel so lucky to have been amazed many times in my career.

I learned how vital it is when encountering those, including ourselves, with perceived challenges, to never reduce an individual to a description of their weaknesses, but instead, to play the detective, to uncover the potential avenues of interest or reward. Experimentation and effectively applying new technology and theories can provide a sense of satisfaction and can benefit all participants.

When I used this speculation on myself, I added the mantra that each day I would produce something new, and make some change. Most days I hold true to that promise just as I hear that the students, staff and graduates, like Victor, of Beverley School, also apparently do.

Does this demand come from something in the mortar, that glue between this building's bricks?

Or does it come from a willingness to live fully and to continuously learn which cradles an acknowledgement of hope and perseverance that is seen again and again in its staff, its students and their parents?

Today, true to my mantra, I have made a change. Today, my art trunks are unpacked and my friends are now freed to remind and to inspire again.

Please note that all paintings (after being photographed) were returned to all my former students who could be located after my retirement in 2007. If anyone knows the whereabouts of any other former art students, particularly Marlene Neto and Leonardo di Salvo, please contact Alana Grossman, Principal, Beverley School.

Group Project

Tile Project

TOY DOCTOR:
PLAYING AND LEARNING AT SUNNY VIEW PS

BY ANNIE APPLEBY

Terona Green came into my family's life in 1988 when we joined Extend-A-Family via the local church. My husband felt that we had energy and love to share and that our two sons needed to learn about the challenges faced by children who are wheelchair-dependent. For the following seven years we involved Terona in our weekend activities and family excursions.

Terona came to birthday parties and had her wheelchair decorated like the bicycles and tricycles of the other guests. She sailed in rafts at wading pools, tobogganed down hills in winter snow, dressed up for Hallowe'en and came to the street parade. Terona taught us that fun at Wonderland was possible for all.

The boys really liked that when she was with us we didn't have to wait in lines; we were escorted through entrances with dignity, consideration and care. This was a mutually beneficial relationship.

This continued until we lost touch due to her family's relocation.

In 2003, I was promoted as the principal of Sunny View Junior and Senior Public School, which serves the needs of elementary students with physical disabilities. The assignment wasn't quite what I had been hoping for as I wanted to work in a regular school in order to promote understanding of children with special education needs. However, this was a perfect match as it married all my backgrounds: nursing, applied psychology and teacher education with special needs and early years' education.

Imagine my surprise when I saw photographs of Terona Green in the albums lovingly kept by the staff at Sunny View. Sadly, I learned that Terona had died from respiratory complications when she was just twenty-one years of age. But her influence on my life continued.

At Sunny View I learned about how to reach and support children whose speech, movement and cognition were compromised. It became a passion for me to structure meaningful activities in art, physical education and play. This led to the creation of the "Toy Doctor" position at the school. Our Toy Doctor, Dale Zimmerman, manufactures and adapts toys and equipment to give access and independence to the children.

A workroom was built in the basement and a partnership established with Dr. Tom Chau at Bloorview MacMillan Kids Rehabilitation Hospital, which resulted in the current Infinity Communication Access Lab.

The Snoezelen Room, funded by twenty Scotiabank branches located in North York, has provided wonderful sensory experiences for the children.

Recently, Rogers showed a film about Sunny View and the amazing work of those who reach and teach children with special needs. Dale Zimmerman, teachers, students and trustee Geri Gershon were profiled as well as the school itself.

Some of the ideas that we incorporated at Sunny View were stimulated by the practices of teachers at Beverley School. Alana and I were part of a principal learning team of six who met monthly. We met to support each other whilst trying to problem-solve the issues faced by students, families and staff, who manage physical and cognitive challenges every day.

I am grateful for my learning journey and the way that my life has been positively affected by the Toy Doctor and creative ideas around access and inclusion. My experience at Sunny View has taken me full circle.

Room 117 Collaboration

Student Group Project

THROUGH YOUR BROTHER'S EYES

BY BECKY QUINLAN

Jack, I want to tell you a story. First of all, you are loved dearly by your family. We want to wrap you up and protect you in this world. We marvel at all the progress you make and celebrate each small milestone you reach. We wish every day that you have a happy life and find a niche where you are safe and valued. For now, that place is Beverley School.

You are special, Jack, and you have a positive impact on those who have the chance to interact with you. Everyone tells me that your sunny disposition brings a light to their life. The world would be a better place if your positive perspective could be shared by all. It's hard to describe your essence, but you radiate sweetness, enthusiasm, brightness and love.

How did you become this wonder?

When you were born, you seemed to be a healthy boy, but you were having trouble feeding. Things grew worse during your first seven weeks of life; you were losing weight and not reaching milestones. They diagnosed you with "failure to thrive," and we ended up in Sick Kids.

Although our first weeks with you had been stressful, we could not have predicted the shock and heartache that would follow as test after test showed anomalies throughout your little body. After three weeks in the hospital, our precious baby had a general diagnosis of Global Developmental Delay and Hypotonia. You had become one of many statistics of genetics, a "medical mystery," and all the expectations of how our lives were going to be were shattered.

Now, you are six years old, and although your development is slow, you continue to make progress as each year goes by. And, even though there has been sadness, your light shines brightly and we prefer to count the blessings that you have brought into our lives.

But, this story isn't about your special charms, Jack. It's supposed to be about your brother Matthew, and how he sees you. Matthew was two years old when you were born, so he doesn't really remember the hospital stay. Over the years, he has become your biggest fan. Matthew loves to play with you and do silly things to make you laugh. He also thinks that you are funny, and he tells stories about you to his friends and teachers. He has been such a good brother that he has let you take over some of his favourite toys like Curious George, his flags, balls, trains, harmonica, even his Nintendo DS (that is, until you kept drooling on it!).

The thing is Jack, you want to do whatever your brother is doing, whether it is building things, playing hockey in the driveway or playing video games. While other big brothers are shooing their pesky little brothers away, Matthew encourages you and finds ways for you to join in. He is also your protector, and makes sure that you are safe. I cannot count the number of times Matt has run to help you if he thought you were going to get hurt in some way (like going up or down the stairs by yourself), or called out to warn me that you were in harm's way. I see how Matthew is with you, and it melts my heart. Again, we count our blessings that there is such a relationship of brotherly love between the two of you.

I also wonder how this special relationship developed.

I don't think we intervened in any way, or explained to Matthew how he should treat you. It seems to have come naturally to him. His perspective is truly amazing, and I think he sees you like no other person in the world does. Only a few times have I heard Matthew refer to the fact that you have some differences. A few years ago, he said to me, "Mom, I know Jack has one leg shorter that the other, but to me they look the same." More recently, I overheard him explain to his friend why you go to Beverley School. "Well, he's missing part of his brain, but he's still really, really smart, and one of his legs is short, but he's still really, really fast."

His comments bring tears to my eyes and joy to my heart. I have never clarified his descriptions of you because his perspective is valid and unique. All he sees is you—his little brother, Jack. His view is not tainted by the opinions of dozens of doctors, the interventions of many therapists, the hundreds of appointments we have attended, the countless tests you have endured. He is just your brother and his role is to help you, nurture you, protect you and above all be your friend and biggest supporter.

So—what is the moral of this story? It's about perspective.

Jack, I hope that you remain the same sweet and joyful person that you are. And Matthew, I hope that your amazing perspective on your brother remains intact. I know that it is a lot to ask, but my dream is that your view of Jack becomes contagious. Is it too much to ask that everyone see children with disabilities as "just kids"? That they should be accepted, included and valued without question? If there was a way for Matthew's outlook to spread, I would rest assured the world could continue to be a happy and safe place for you. In the meantime, Jack, keep sharing your light with the world, and Matthew, continue sharing your life with your brother. At least we have our own small niche where true acceptance, happiness and love has been achieved.

Maddie

LESSONS FROM MADDIE

BY CHERYL FORD

I had never lived with or spent time with anyone with a disability before we were blessed with Madison, thirteen and a half years ago. I have nursed many people who had life-altering injuries but Madison is a whole new experience that has taught me more than I could ever have imagined.

I have learned that someone who never speaks a word can say volumes. You just have to be patient and "listen" by watching for visual cues. Then there is her zest for life, her appreciation of simple pleasures like feeling the wind or the sun or even a gentle rain on her face. Courage is another lesson I've learned; like the other students at school, Madison is a true example of courage. Life itself is challenging for Madison and yet she, like so many of her classmates, has a very sunny disposition and finds it easy to love others unconditionally.

Madison has some defining characteristics like her laugh and her hugs. Maddie has the most contagious laugh, a full body from the belly kind of laugh. Then there are her "squeezy" hugs, a sort of a pulsating hug that sometimes goes on for some time. When Madison hugs you, you know for certain you have gotten a good hug; sometimes you feel like you have also gotten chiropractic treatment. When Maddie is excited she often does a little dance and laughs. This can happen with the slightest provocation and it is a head-bobbing ricocheting-off-your-belly laugh till your-face-falls-off kind of dance.

"Raspberries," are another trait she is well known for. Let me illustrate with a little story of an event that took place in November on a class field trip to Allen Gardens.

My husband and I like to go on these trips as we enjoy being with the class. I was not able to go, but Doug was happy to be there. I had arranged to meet them at Allen Gardens after the field trip because Maddie had an appointment, and we were going to leave from there.

I walked over to Allen Gardens to meet them; I went through the cactus greenhouse looking for a large group of wheelchairs, only to find none. I moved on to the next greenhouse, still no wheelchairs. Finally, I strolled into the last greenhouse, still not finding what I was looking for. Then, just as I was starting to wonder where they had gone, and if I had gotten the day mixed up or was at the wrong place, I heard the sound of raspberries coming through the leaves. I knew that sound and knew I had found at least one person that I was looking for, so I followed the sound of the "raspberry." Sure enough, as I rounded the corner and looked through the leaves, I found Doug and Maddie sitting on a bench enjoying the greenery around them. "Raspberries" are a trait that some find annoying but others, like the pastor at our church, quite enjoy; he especially appreciates it when Madison punctuates his sermons with a good raspberry.

There is another story that I just have to share with you. Several years ago, we took a trip to Disney World. On our return home, we sat in the airport waiting lounge for a long time, so just before boarding the flight I thought it a good idea to take Maddie to the bathroom, hoping that in so doing, I would avoid having to use the bathroom on the plane; we all know how very spacious they are. Mission accomplished and we boarded the plane.

We were sitting in the aircraft for what seemed like an eternity, waiting on the tarmac to be cleared for takeoff. It was then that it became apparent Madison needed another washroom break. I tried to convince myself that this was just not possible because we had just been there. Madison has impeccable timing.

Of course there was nothing we could do except to sit back and hope that the aircraft would get off the ground ASAP; finally, with a roar we were in the air. But the seatbelt sign seemed to take forever to turn off. In the meantime, I tried to convince myself that this was just a false alarm. Finally, the seatbelt sign was turned off.

Here we go, grab the backpack, extricate myself and Madison from the seat and head down the aisle. As we start down the aisle the backpack falls off my shoulder and unfortunately both of my hands are occupied. I cannot put it back up on my shoulder, so it ends up hitting a few people on the head as we pass them. I profusely apologize and carry on.

Finally, we get to the little room in the back; the sardine can that is only big enough for one sardine. I now proceed to shoehorn two sardines into the can…whew…success…we are both in and the door closes.

What now? Neither one of us has room to sit down, so we do the hokey-pokey and we give ourselves a shake and I have somehow managed to get her seated in the right place. At this point in time, both of us are upright but soon, in order to change her pants, one of us is going to need to stand on our head (that would be me). Oh, oh…this is the tricky bit in the sardine can. I manage to stand on my head and change her pants. Then I hear that dreaded sound, "pong, pong, pong." The seatbelt sign is back on and we hit turbulence. Now the sardine can resembles a cocktail shaker; shaken, not stirred.

Okay, next step: dispose of the waste. Oh, but the opening is just big enough for a tissue, not a diaper. "Pong, pong, pong." That blinkin' alarm is still on and, yes I know, I have to get back to my seat but I still have one more task—getting clean clothes on Madison in the cocktail shaker/sardine can. Here goes: two of us, one upright and one standing on her head, flying around inside the washroom and by some magical feat, I manage to get her pants on and put her back together.

We are now ready to brave the turbulence and the plane pitching around in order to get to our seat. Thankfully the crew, who were eating their lunch in the back of the aircraft, were very helpful in providing garbage bags and picking up lost shoes on the way back to our seat. Phew, what an excursion.

Lessons learned: Always be prepared for anything; always take not one, but two, garbage bags and always take a change of clothes. I think we both preferred the larger washroom with a little less motion. Hey, it was fun while it lasted but not nearly as fun as the rides at Disney.

I think I need a stiff drink and then a nap.

I wouldn't trade all of the wonderful experiences and challenges we have had with Madison for the world. I am a much different and much better person for knowing Maddie; she teaches me about what is truly important in life. She teaches me to enjoy the small but significant things in life that make it rich and wonderful.

Here's to you, Maddie. You rock!!

Room 117 Collaboration

Beverley Summer School project

MICHAEL

BY CHRISTINE MARTENS

Years ago, when I just started working at Beverley, I had a student named Michael. He was quite immobile, unable to move even his head. He tended to stare slightly upward and show a limited, if any, response to others.

Sometimes I would take Michael out of his chair and support him sitting upright next to me with my arm around his shoulders. I told him we were going to the movies together. I would read to him and do hand-over-hand work with him as well.

Michael wasn't able to show much in the way of expression, so it was hard to tell if anything we did with him was making an impact.

One day, I was just returning from my lunch break when I saw our principal sitting next to Michael with a book. I said, "Hiya Michael," and his face lit up with a big smile. We were both shocked and thrilled at the same time.

Michael passed away about a year later. I'd already attended a few funerals for students who had passed on, but Michael was the only one I dared go up to and stroke his hair like I used to.

People may not have seen a lot of life in Michael as he lived, but he certainly filled a hole in my life that I will never forget.

God bless you, Michael.

Tile Project

ROBERT

BY CHRISTINE MARTENS

There was a student named Robert who was quite bright and a little mischievous. He couldn't speak because of a tracheotomy, and so he breathed through a plastic tube in his neck.

Robert loved to watch cars on the street and would often flip over the wagons in the open area to check underneath them. I figured he was aspiring to become an auto mechanic.

One day in the change room, I had Robert support himself while standing at the change table. I decided to also change the towel he wore around his neck and ended up removing it faster than I meant to. I realized, too late, that I had also pulled out his tracheotomy valve. Robert fell down on top of me and I yelled out for someone to call 911. As a number of people were calling the office at the same time, our nurse, Linda, came in to see what was wrong. I thought Robert was dying in my arms. In tears, I told her what had happened.

Linda calmly looked at me and said that Robert was still breathing through the hole in his neck and it would be a number of hours before it closed up.

I then noticed Robert looking up at me, and the sound that I thought was him crying was, in fact, laughter. He had a huge smile on his face and was making happy wheezing sounds through the hole in his neck.

Well, that was one way to learn not to jump to conclusions.

Eyob

HARD TO SOFT

BY DAVE ASQUINI

As a caretaker, my first day at Beverley School was a total change in culture. I was used to working high schools, where everyone minds their own business and keeps a thick skin, where people look out for themselves. Walking into here, I was welcomed into a community. It isn't policies or politics—it's all about the children.

This is the first school I worked in a school where everyone came up to me, introduced themselves and asked me what my name was. I've been here five years, and by far, it's the best school in the school board. I've never met a group of staff as dedicated to the children as they are in this school. I've never seen a group of parents as dedicated to a school. Every one of the families shows up, and what's more important, everyone has a say.

Walking through here each day, and being able to see all the projects and artwork the kids have worked on, is an amazing feeling. Seeing how far the students have come, seeing them with new technologies, like iPads, you can feel that these kids are better off here than at other places.

Beverley School has a principal who will defend these kids and this school until the end. You don't see that a lot, because many people in this world are here for a paycheque. Walking through Beverley School you notice, this building is well kept and cleaner than most, and we have the cleanest floors, as seen on CBS's *60 Minutes!* Even work orders are filled within weeks. It's a warm, relaxed atmosphere, people talk, people communicate, people talk to you like a person, not a number, not a personnel number.

When I first came here, I was like the Grinch, and like the Grinch, my heart grew five times bigger. The first student I ever met was Nuno. He was eating his lunch at a blue table, and I've never seen a student at a school who was as happy as he was. There was one teacher whose students were all in wheelchairs. She said how much she wanted to bring her students around the world to see different countries. I suggested she make up some passports and go, so she did! She showed them videos from around the world, read them stories, and stamped their passports as they travelled the world from within the classroom. I've never been a creative person. As a caretaker, I can either mop like this, or like that. But it felt cool to see an idea of mine come to life and benefit the students. That's the kind of place this is.

Class Project

Classroom Project

CAMP COUCHICHING

BY DAVID CAMPOS

I didn't like kids. I didn't like the outdoors. But when I was twenty, and my friend asked me if I wanted a summer job at his camp, I shrugged my shoulders and agreed that there were worse ways to spend a summer. Soon enough, I was enjoying being a counsellor at Camp Couchiching, so when asked if I wanted to provide one-on-one support for a camper with special needs, I shrugged my shoulders and agreed once again.

When I first met Karl, I thought I had made a huge mistake. Karl was nine, but he couldn't run very fast or jump very high. He couldn't even really talk much. He had seizures all the time and took medication that made him sluggish and difficult to understand. I didn't know what to do.

I quickly learned that Karl didn't sleep very much, either. Every night, Karl would stay up late and shine his flashlight under his sleeping bag, make noise with his books, and annoy the other campers in the cabin. After four sleepless nights, I was at my wits end. I remember dragging myself out of my bed at three o'clock in the morning and demanding that Karl put away his flashlight and books.

When he screamed and refused, I demanded to know what it was about this junky old flashlight and tattered book he liked so much. But Karl didn't have the words to explain, so instead, he very deliberately flipped to a page in his favourite book and shone the flashlight on a passage that read, "Everything the light touches is part of your kingdom." I believe he granted me a rare and generous look into his world.

When I think about Karl and all the other campers in that program, it makes me feel so fortunate that I got to spend time with a very special population of kids that I wouldn't ordinarily get the opportunity to meet. Several years later, I did a university placement in Karl's class, and now I am completing my eighth year as a very proud special education teacher.

I think that one of the most admirable qualities in a human being is their willingness to care for someone who has difficulty caring for themselves, despite the struggle. Camp taught me that.

I decided to share some of the joys and lessons of camp by organizing a school-wide overnight field trip to Camp Couchiching for the students of Beverley. The trip involved the effort of all my colleagues, wheelchair buses and family members of students. The resulting smiles and laughter during camp activities and outdoor games and a bonfire, was my way of passing along a powerful experience that shaped me as a person and as a teacher.

Group Project

Classroom Project

SAUL

BY DAVID ROLFE

"Pee pee on the pot-tee, pee pee on the pot-tee," I sing.

Saul lowers his gaze from the ceiling to meet mine.

Great, I think—eye contact.

"Pee pee on the pot-tee, pee pee on the pot-tee."

He shifts slightly on the toilet. He's a big boy for a seven-year-old, but sitting on an adult toilet seat is still a logistical challenge. I try one more time, waiting for him to chime in. The hint of a smile appears on his round face.

"Pee pee on the pod-dee, pee pee on the pod-dee," he joins in now. "Pee pee on the pod-dee."

Together we sing two more rounds. Nothing.

"Do you need to pee?" I ask. Before I can finish the sentence I hear a faint sound in the toilet.

"Good job," I say. I throw my arms up in the air in celebration and give him a smile, but he's already standing and struggling to pull up his underwear. I move my chair back to give him room. He turns around and flushes. One of his shoes has fallen off and without bending over he's attempting to slip his foot in.

"Do you need help?" I finish the sentence by signing Help.

"Help," he says.

Together we work on the getting-the-foot-actually-in-the-shoe routine. With the runners mostly on, he shuffles past me towards the sink. Or so I think.

I hear a giggle as he accelerates and runs towards the nearest bean bag chair in the classroom.

Didn't wash his hands. Again.

Tomorrow is another day, I think.

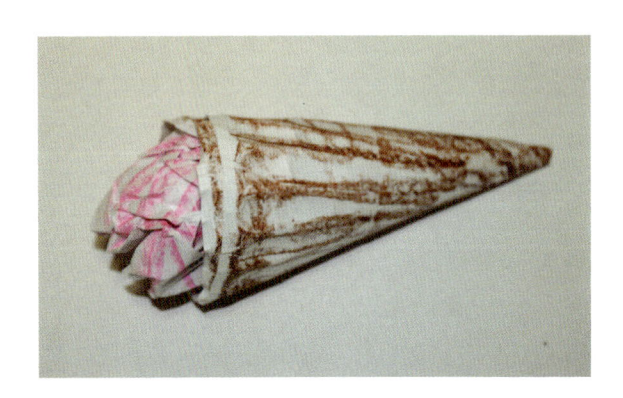

BLESSED

BY DENNIS THOMSON

The woman from whom we rented the apartment lived above us and was a single mom whose two children were six and eight years old. Her son, the elder child, in later years, was diagnosed with Asperger's syndrome.

He's in his mid-twenties now and is taking a reduced course load at a university. He lives in her basement apartment under her supervision, while he learns the skills to lead an independent life. To recall him as a withdrawn, non-verbal, hand-flapping child, to see him now as an adult journeying to independence, is a testament to the untiring advocacy, love and energy of his mother. That we should all be so blessed.

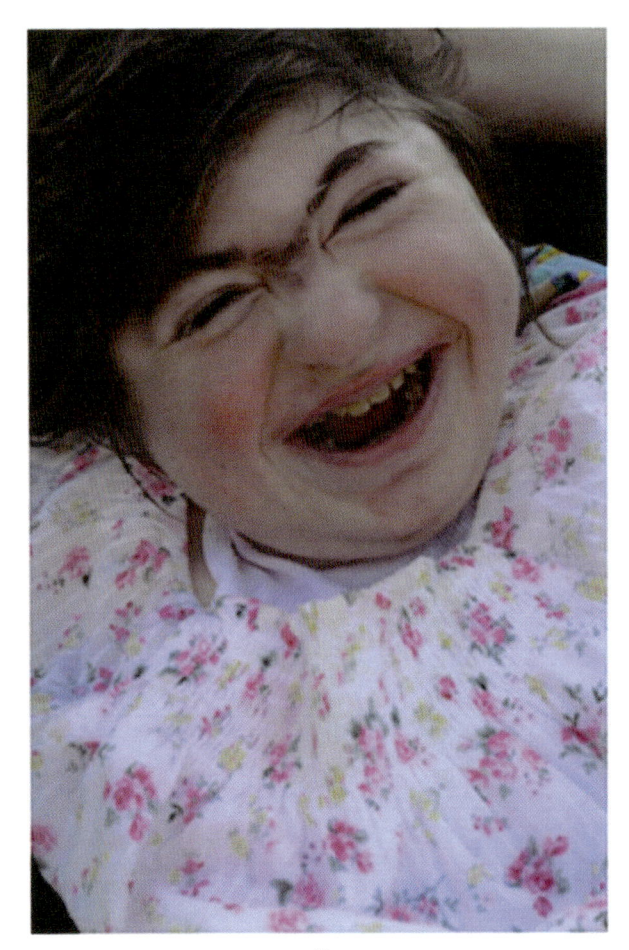

Madison

LET ME INTRODUCE YOU TO MADISON

BY DOUG FORD

Throughout the pregnancy there was no indication that there were any major problems. Then at two a.m., after she was born, my wife was awakened by the doctor who said that Madison had some "interesting features." Now there is a loaded statement. It was then that we learned Madison had a heart problem. Later she would be diagnosed with Toriello-Carey syndrome; at the time, Madison was one of about twelve children in the world with this syndrome. I know that every parent thinks that their child is special, but Madison has just about everyone else beaten!

After the doctor came to see my wife and gave her "the news," things started coming at us thick and fast: various consulting doctors, feeding specialists, social workers and the list kept getting longer. We started a binder to keep track of all the people caring for Madison. Madison wasn't even six weeks old when we were transferred to a large teaching hospital. There was an endless parade through Madison's room. It seemed like every medical service in the hospital was consulted. Ironically, she was supposed to be resting up for cardiac surgery.

What struck us was how the humanity of medicine, in a few cases, was some way lost. Cheryl, my wife, recounts how the Genetics team, when they came in to see Madison, did not address Madison or even Cheryl, who was in the room at the time. They simply removed Madison's bed clothes, gown and diaper, then they pointed out every defect that Madison had. When they were done, they simply left the room and left Madison lying there naked, looking like road kill.

Madison did get her heart surgery, we did get her home, and along the way we did meet a great many doctors, nurses and allied health professionals who were fabulous and cared for us well.

Both my wife and I are neuroscience nurses (how ironic) and now we had a newborn with a neurologic syndrome. As we look back on the first night at home with Madison, Cheryl and I can now laugh. Madison was lying in a bassinet in the middle of the kitchen floor; Cheryl and I were thinking, okay, now what? Just then Madison barfed and not just a little burp but rather full-on projectile vomit; she had a range of three feet. Now bear in mind, we did not get any instruction about what to expect from a new baby and to neuroscience nurses, projectile vomiting is a bad thing. You could hear the alarm bells going off in our heads as we sprang to action stations—Airway, Breathing, Circulation, Check Pupil Response—because on a newborn that is about all we could wring out of the Glasgow Coma Scale. Thus began our journey with Madison who is now thirteen years old.

Madison is about to graduate from elementary school, a feat no one could have foreseen when Madison came into this world. We heard a lot of gloom and doom along the way, but with a lot of courage, fortitude and a strong support network of family, church, school and health care providers, Madison has come light years beyond what was expected of her at the beginning of her life.

Tile Project

Student Photos with Alexander Sam

LESSONS

BY ELLEN SCHWARTZ

When asked to participate in Beverley Writes, I was taken back to a speech that I had prepared for the Toronto District School Board's personal development day: "Here's a little lesson from Beverley school." This is the speech.

When Alana Grossman, principal of Beverley School, asked me to come and speak to you, I thought to myself "What can I teach this group of special, special teachers that they haven't taught me?"

When we think of Special Education, we think of the children who fall into this very unique category.

Today I am going to speak to you about the love, appreciation and great respect of who you are and the importance of what you do on a daily basis!

Years ago, before Jeff and I were married, we were asked to play in a ball hockey game at Bloorview. That was the first time that I had been exposed to anyone with severe and complex disabilities. We walked into the Bloorview gymnasium and I was introduced to this ten-year-old little boy. He was confined to a wheelchair and was surrounded by tubes and pumps. He held his deformed hand up to mine to try to touch it. My heart melted and I felt like sobbing. I was to be his eyes and legs for the game. I tried to mask my fear and discomfort, but had no idea how to talk to someone who couldn't speak back.

A smile never left his face. Tears never left mine.

Little did I know that I would mother a very similar child.

You see I didn't know then, but I know now, that inclusion isn't about opening up our world for people with special needs. Inclusion is about people with special needs teaching us what life is all about.

Our son Jacob has a rare neurodegenerative illness called Canavan disease. We were told that he would never be able to walk, talk, see, eat by mouth, or live to his fourth birthday. At the time of Jake's diagnosis, Jeff and I had thought our lives had ended, but as you all know…our life was just beginning.

Jacob is now fifteen. He is a student at Beverley School now for nine years.

I still remember that transition to Beverley. The principal at the time, Terry Tater, informed me that Jacob was to be picked up at eight-thirty a.m. We had never let Jacob out of our sight.

I thought she was mad!

The first week, every day I followed the van all the way downtown until Jacob had safely reached Beverley School.

Lesson 1 learned: Let go! He will be okay, actually better off!!!

Jacob was loved. He was taken care of. He was happy! I went back to work! All of a sudden, I had a life, and became a much better mom.

Jeff and I used to coddle Jacob. We treated him like a porcelain doll. We held him carefully, kissed him lightly and spoke softly in his presence. We expected everyone else to follow these rules. Well, the staff at Beverley School wanted no part of this. In we walked to visit Jakey. Stacie yelled across the room, "Hey Jake, look who's here." She clutched the sides of Jacob's ribs while he was sitting in his wheelchair and she started rubbing and shaking her hands. A massive smile overcame his face. "Wait until you see his happy feet!"

He had no idea what she had intended for us. All of a sudden Jakey's feet shot up in the air in reaction to the delight that he was feeling.

"See, these are his happy feet!"

That day Stacie taught us.

Stacie introduced an entirely new way to communicate with Jacob. This was one lesson that we have shared with so many.

Lesson 2: He won't break!!

The teachers at Beverley taught us our most valuable lesson on Jacob's birthday on May 17th.

On a hot spring day, we came in to visit on Jake's birthday. The birthday boy waited in his tumble form, flaunting off his yellow crown fit for a king. In front of him was a homemade birthday cake with JAKE written in whipped cream on the top.

His teachers were all waiting for us to sing happy birthday. Together we all sang to our miracle birthday boy. Alex, his teacher at the time, said in a slow but determined voice,"Jacob, blow out your birthday candles."

Jeff and I looked at each other with a reluctant and questioning gaze. "There is no way he can do this, why is she making this command?"

Again, slowly she commanded, "Jacob, please blow out your candles."

Alex guided Jacob's hand to a large red button. She eased his hand on top of the button and pressed down. This accelerated a fan which began to turn. Jacob blew out his candles!

This has become our family motto. Whatever we do and wherever we go, Jacob does it too!

Most other boys go to camp, Jacob does too.

Most other boys go swimming, Jacob does too.

Most other boys play ball hockey with the street kids, try getting a goal past Jacob when he is blocking the net!

Most other boys get to rock climb, so does Jacob, with a counsellor on a ladder holding his head up.

Most Jewish boys have a bar mitzvah, so did Jacob.

Lesson 3: It's not "if" Jacob will do things, it's how!!

A principal friend of mine told me this story. She had a friend who taught grade one. She asked her class of six-year-olds to draw a picture of a "happy day." Most children drew pictures with a yellow sun, bright flowers, smiles on faces, etc.. One boy drew a sombre picture. His picture had a dark purple landscape with brown flowers, a black sun and dark blue clouds.

The teacher was concerned and she called in the principal. The principal called in the parents. The parents called in the psychologist. Something must be wrong. Finally, they all brought in the child to ask a few questions.

They asked, "Why is it that when you were asked to draw a picture of a happy day, your day was filled with so many dark colours? Is everything okay?"

"Well Miss Jones, when you have us draw, you pass around that big box of crayons. I sit in the last seat in the last row, so by the time it gets to me, those are the only colours that are left."

Many adults impose our adult interpretations on children's behaviours.

I share this story now, because with you, special special teachers, this wouldn't happen. You ask the child first and then involve the parents if needed.

You interpret our children's interpretations and impose them on our adult behaviours!

In our recent IPRC (a parent's favourite thing!), we spoke about Jacob's needs when he graduates from Beverley, a place he has called home for nine years.

I put on my strong face and went into the meeting. I sat down in the chair and sobbed. So much for being strong.

We spoke about Jacob's needs. Linda, Jacob's teacher, started rhyming off Jacob's facial expressions and what they all mean. "Oo, when he sticks his tongue out, it means that he is uncomfortable." She can read his signs and catch every cue. He has never uttered a word, but she speaks his language.

Because of teachers like you, a life that could have been tragic and sad, has become enlightening and full. As you teach Jacob and us, he teaches the world.

Student Textures Project

Madison's Life

A true story
By: Emma
ilestrated by: Emma

Hi I'm maddie

Madison has a very good life living here in toronto. She has a nice family, nice doctors and nice friends at her school. She has Lots of good food. She learns alot at home and at school. She has her own iPad 2 she has stuff on the iPad so she can learn stuff too. maddie has a seperet Room then her sister Emma they have seperet rooms. on

Sundays Emma, her, mom. and ~~her~~ Dad go to church the perents stay upstairs while the kids go downstairs to Sunday school we do crafts downstairs and we do memory verses too. On weekdays maddie gose to scool so dose Emma. She has to take a bus to go to school and Emma dose not. Every day after school we all have a snack Maddie has left over snack from the day before. Me Emma and maddie play before dinner when over mom calls we have to get ready for dinner maddie eats in her wheelchair or her red chair it depends on maddie. Then after dinner we have a bath then a story then we go to bed. on Wensday maddie has a worker her name is Kathrine. On thursday maddie has dinner with marline she is nice to maddie and me, my mom and my dad. Every friday Nodie One comes to work

with maddie. Maddie has
the whole day with
her family on friday.
Maddie and Emma play
Bairbies or puppy lily.
Maddie likes to play
puppy lily that is her
favourite game. Maddies
favourite food is chilie her
favourite movie is toy story
1. Maddies favourite coloor
is purpple. She Loves
her family and ouer
family pet fish chatolotte
she loves her bed she
has a warm red bed.
she loves mostly a

everything exep shots flue shots. not like she those dose it hurts for her she loves everything

the end

P.S two things I like about maddie is she loves to dance and she loves musicl

Classroom Project

Painting by Leonard

DANCING OUR WAY TO INTEGRATION

BY FRANCES BERMAN

Too many times, congregated schools are criticized for not offering their students an integrated opportunity. However, too many times in integrated schools, the DD population, those with a developmental disability, is ignored and meaningful integration never takes place.

In the fall of 2002, a reverse integration program was established between some of the special needs students at Park Lane School with typically developing students in a grade two class at Owen Public School. Once a week, during the fall and spring months, the Owen students travelled to Park Lane to participate in wheelchair folk dancing. Prior to their initial visit, I went to Owen with my physiotherapist and a companion wheelchair to talk to the children about the new friends they were going to be meeting. Even with preparation, the initial dance session was a bit of a shock for the Owen students, but come the spring, they could hardly wait to come back and dance with their new friends. A daytime recital was held at each school in the spring for students and parents.

The following year, the program expanded to include two classes from Owen. Parents were thrilled to have their children involved in the program, and specifically requested that their child be in the grade two class that was involved in the wheelchair dancing program.

Two years later, John Fisher Public School became involved so we had two classes from Owen and two classes from John Fisher coming to Park Lane to folk dance. The enthusiasm was contagious! And with that enthusiasm came the creation of the Special Needs Folk Fest—a dance festival where able-bodied children danced with the special needs partners.

Initially, there were about six or eight schools and classes involved in the festival, which was held in the spring at East York Collegiate. But the festival grew and grew until the school's gym could no longer accommodate the program. At that point, the festival moved to Ted Reeves Arena and in a few short years, the Folk Fest has outgrown that facility as well!

When the program was created in 2002, the sole purpose was good pedagogy. I also wanted to demystify and take away the fear that many people have of individuals with special needs. Do it at an early age—before the seeds of preconceived notions are planted.

When I retired from Park Lane, my one wish was to have the reverse integration program continue and culminate in the Special Needs Folk Fest.

Here it is, five years later. Some of the players have changed but the program just keeps on growing with more schools getting involved as we continue to dance our way to integration.

Frances Berman,
Principal (Retired)
Park Lane School

Group Mobile Project

Classroom Project

ONCE UPON A NIECE

BY HEIDI MITCHELL

We're a working title for a really long book. And, if it came too easy, it wouldn't be worth all the time that it took.

- Davey von Bohlen

It's a fact: studies have found that exposure is the one of best indicators of positive attitudes and acceptance. Seriously, it's true; I've seen the research, read the articles, can produce the statistical results. For this reason, I am grateful that from the time I was just a tot I was "exposed." People with disabilities have enriched my life for as long as I can remember. When I was only six, my parents volunteered at a long-term care facility for children with developmental disabilities near my hometown.

One Saturday morning, I was waiting on a bench in the lobby while my mom talked to some staff. A young man sat down beside me, too close, and leaned his face right into mine looking at me from the corner of his eyes. Oh...my...God, I thought. Hello, personal space! I considered getting up and hightailing it out of there, but I sat perfectly still. I figured he was just curious and really, so was I. That was the first time I came face-to-face (literally!) with disability.

By the time I was in high school I was on the path to making a career of it. Even so, when disability showed up on my doorstep, neither book-learning nor hours-logged prepared me.

Unlike scholarly reports, fairy tales usually take place long, long ago in a faraway land. Although this story isn't a fable and it takes place in the not-too-distant past and relatively nearby, something magical did happen.

Once upon a time, a young woman received news that her sister-in-law was with child.

The woman purchased a stamp, sent a Hallmark card and life unfolded as it should. In case you didn't pick up on this, that woman was me. Something else you may not know (hopefully!) is that I'm kind of a horrible person. Yup. Case in point: when my brother's wife announced that she was pregnant I was...underwhelmed. After all, it didn't really impact my life. They lived a million kilometers down the 401, give or take. I'd see the new addition on holidays, but my day-to-day would remain unchanged. The rest of the world had a much more socially acceptable response. Friends, colleagues, people I hardly knew came up to me and exclaimed with all the enthusiasm of a kid on Christmas: you must be so excited about becoming an aunt! Um, sure.

The months flew by, showers were thrown and eventually the big day came. My niece was born on a balmy afternoon in June. Three weeks late. I got a text from my brother, Erick, telling me that my sister-in-law, Erin, had gone into labour, but then hours passed and there was no new news. In this particular instance, no news was not good news. My mom phoned that evening and asked me to call my brother. Her voice was quiet and strange. I didn't ask why the request. I just knew I should do it.

I called. He picked up the phone and there was silence on the other end of the line. I waited. It was the first time I heard my brother cry. I mean really cry. Worst sound ever. The words he was saying all made perfectly intelligible sentences. Nouns, verbs, subjects, no split infinitives but, surely, they couldn't be right. This was the point at which an older sister was supposed to say something supportive. Reassuring. Curative. Absolving. Deny the accuracy of the statement like a Harvard-trained lawyer. Powerless, I repeated the words: it doesn't matter what anybody says, she's perfect; until they disintegrated in my mouth like gum chewed for too long.

On what should have been the happiest day of their lives (so far), a young couple was shattered by the words of a man in scrubs. Words repeated in hushed tones to closest family only. Words that conveyed a different message to each listener.

Erin heard blame. What did she do? Did she take over-the-counter drugs? A glass of wine before she knew she was pregnant? She was in the house when Erick painted the nursery. But, she had followed the doctor's orders to a tee. Why, then? In the past year almost every one of their friends had had a baby with no complications. Every one. How was this fair?

Erick heard implausibility. She seems fine, doesn't she? How do we get a second opinion? What would it mean if Erin couldn't go back to work because the baby required special care? Not to mention what that might cost.

My mother, for all her experiences and open-mindedness, heard words that invoked fear. She stayed in the background. Facial lines in a furrowed brow of concern, rather than in the laughter and smiles at the birth of her first grandchild. A grandma at arm's length.

The very next day, I made the trip up to see Bailey. I cried the whole long drive to our hometown hospital. My tears caused me considerable distress. I spend forty hours a week with children with disabilities and love every minute of it. What was I crying about? How many awesome kids have I met? Why should news of my niece be met with such sorrow? I was a hypocrite. A poseur.

My visit seemed like a duty: go in, observe niece, provide feedback and suggestions. But instead, when I held her, I heard something myself. I heard a sound that started out low and steadily grew. I heard: it's okay. The words I had spoken were true: she was perfect. Maybe it was the ray of cuteness coming from her crystal blue eyes, like some kind of infant superhero (the Amazing Bailey Bee!) that made me fall crazy in love. Who knows? I know this: an aunt was born.

Initially, I felt engaged because I thought Bailey needed me, but I quickly realized that I needed her. We needed her. To bring us together as a complete family for the first time since my father died. My little brother all grown up, Erin a beaming mama and, of course, proud (and now, slightly less horrible) Aunt Heidi. I never could have imagined it was possible to love someone else's kid so much.

These days, we all get the same message. Usually, it's "more juice." The weekly visits to the children's hospital have trickled down to check-ins at fixed intervals, getting further and further apart. Please don't misunderstand; it's scary not knowing what might happen down the road. It's hard not being able to predict her future. But, honestly, can anyone ever do that?

This story is short, since most of it is still unwritten. But, I'm going to ruin the ending for you:

Happily ever after is guaranteed...

Tile Project

Jake

JAKE'S STORY: 1

BY JAKE LIGHTFOOT

This is the first of two stories dictated by one of our students and transcribed by staff. The stories were told over the course of an hour-long swim class.

Back in the cage!
Ahhh I'm falling! Ahhh I'm falling!
Gotta catch him.
We have no time to lose everyone!
Woo woo vote for me.
That's really high, we can't climb up there.
Get back get bubbles pants up pants up.
Daddy? Can you hear me?
TWO LASERS! TWO LASERS!
Ooooooooooo ai Yai yai
No I'm not better than you! No I'm not better than you! Oh ya oh ya!?
I escaped.
What are those guys doing there? There were five now there are four…
One went away to go hide, now there are three.
1, 2, 3, 4, 5, 6, 7, 8. 9, 10. YA! Now it's time to play.
One went away now there are three.
Whoa out of the way. Take it away Jay.

I work, time for swimming, time to get dressed, time to eat snack, time to get playing, time to goodbye circle.

Wow! Jonah where did you get the new shirt?

Bye have fun at school. Say bye have fun at school.

Paddypaddy hello wuzzat?

Uh oh! There is a hole!

bumbumbeebum lalalalalala

Do you see my clothes? Oooh? I'll show you a red dress that isn't yours. Bro man did you take my clothes? Bro man where's my clothes?... I have my own, I don't need to take yours.

Let go of Harfan! They're coming to get us...bad guys! What do I do? What do I do?

What are you saying?

Did you see my clothes? Yes?

You're not supposed to be up there.

Jonah can't move, he cannot hop backwards. Follow the powers, I know. Into the stairs.

Fourteen...five.... We're turning around in circles!

HIYA HIYA!

Student Photos with Alexander Sam

Classroom Project

JAKE'S STORY: 2

BY JAKE LIGHTFOOT

This is the second of two stories dictated by one of our students and transcribed by staff. The stories were told over the course of an hour-long swim class. Brackets denote a response from staff.

Help I cannot I cannot! Whoa wow.

Going down to the water. Back to the sea.

Rah rah blap blap.

I'm drowning! I got it. I'm coming, I'm coming gunna catch you!

Run run over there!

The man he's getting away! Get him again!

Up and down. Tell Billy. Tell Billy wshoo wshoo he's scared.

Tell me more then. Hooooooooold on.

Wow have a great time. I can't wait to tell mommy I had a great day at school. Mommy I had a great day at school. Oh did you have a great day?

I had a great day at school. I have a kinder egg at home. 1, 2, 1, 2.

I can't wait to tell Mommy. Bwahahaha.

Hey I don't smell it.

Bye bye Mister Man.

(Oh am I leaving?)

Yes.

(Okay. Bye.)

No, over there by the chair. [Jake directs staff like we're actors in his play]

Hey you mister Bob!...Bye Bye MISTER MAN!

(Oh yes, sorry, bye!)

Where's he going? Around the block?

You have to stay here.

(I have to stay here, sure thing.)

HE'S GOING TO CRASH watch out! [I walked into another staff] BWAHAHA.

Take that on this side lady. Mister lady here in the chair.

[Tells staff to sit in the pool lift chair]

He won't listen.

Hawhoo watch me win.

Bye bye mister man. Bye bye mister lady.

Now what are we going to do?

Bye Bye you're leaving.

(Again? Where am I going? Around the block?)

Ya.

Now what are we going to do? I'm amazing! What are we gunna do? NEXT!

What's the man and lady doing?

I'll get Gary. Splash!

Scratch pop yup. What's Harfan doing?

I'm telling Gary. I'll get him. No you watch.

I'll get him I'll get him. He's getting away down under the water. YES!

I got him. [Gets a toy off the bottom]

I got Winnie the Pooh and Tigger out! [clap, clap, clap]

Jonah's supposed to be here.

You're not supposed to be there the man is. [To the instructor sitting in the lifeguard's chair]

The man come see! No stop right here. [He makes me stay for a minute while he laughs]

The keys the keys! I don't know where they are.

(I don't know where they are. Jake, can you find the keys?)

I got it I got them! Splash! [He points to the keys on the floor and laughs]

(Thank you very much)

I got them. I got it. Ummm the ball the ball. Yes I got it.

What's happening next?

Student puzzle piece project

Majeed

THE LION SLEEPS TONIGHT

BY JAMES CONNOR

After a glorious summer at my cottage by the lake, it was time to return for another school year and focus on a new batch of students. It was a great class, great kids, and a great teacher. However, one student had not joined us yet. He would not be arriving until the end of September, as he was out of the country with his family. I had spent the entire summer filled with dread at the prospect of working with this boy. Although I had never worked directly with him before, in previous years I had the opportunity to observe him and his interaction, having worked in a neighbouring class with a shared washroom for the students.

I had many preconceived notions about this boy. Regardless of his autism, or any other factors, I had come to the unwavering conclusion that he was a BRAT. I have no patience for brats. I never have. My sister was a brat and, in my opinion, as an adult she still is. I can sympathize with a genuine outpouring of distress, and I am easily able to discern one from the other, but I have no time for theatrics or insincere manipulation, of any kind.

I would have to be prepared. I would have to set a precedent from the start. I set up a red time-out chair with his name on it. I was going to nip this behaviour in the bud.

Finally, the day came. He arrived on the yellow school bus, and as I prepared to board, I took a deep breath and counted to ten. It was time.

As I made my way toward his seat, I could feel his presence. He occupied the space around him as royalty might. He was in control, a law unto himself, ready to challenge those who might question his will.

As I unclipped his safety belt, he briefly looked up at me and made eye contact in an unconcerned manner, as though my presence was incidental and insignificant. Then he turned away, emitting a low growl under his breath.

"Good morning!" I said.

He did not acknowledge me in any detectable way.

We made our way into the school, and as we approached the classroom, his growling became louder, and his body language more defiant. Upon entering the room, he was greeted by the other staff, who he ignored. He started to march around the room, taking in the surroundings. I directed him to the coat rack, and stated that it was time to take off our coats and hang them on the hook. And so it began. The wails of defiance, the thrashing and tensing of limbs, and the thrusting of the head into the air.

As he tried to brush past me several times, I redirected him back to the coat rack and repeated, "Coat off." He continued to wail and stomp his feet. I was not going to retreat. I repeated, "Coat off," and demonstrated by taking off my hoodie and hanging it on the hook. The defiance continued. As the noise factor escalated, I determined that it was disruptive to the other students and decided to take the exercise out into the hall.

Thanks to an accommodating teacher, who was on board with the idea that focused persistence was the best way to achieve the goal, and who allowed me to take as much time as needed, I pressed on.

I isolated us from the passers-by, in an attempt to direct his focus on me, and placed his hand on the zipper, and repeated, "Coat off." This went on for a good hour, while he continued to scream and stomp his feet. I felt like giving up several times, thinking I was being unreasonable and that I would never win. But I pressed on. I was determined.

Finally, in one glorious moment of absolute frustration and defeat, he reached for his zipper, and in one sharp motion tugged the zipper down to the waistline of his coat. SUCCESS! I then assisted him by pulling it the rest of the way. "GOOD!" I exclaimed. "Now," I said, "take it off."

More resistance followed. A few minutes later, in another fit of rage, he quickly pulled off the coat and threw it at me. "EXCELLENT! You did it! See how easy that was?" I decided that we had accomplished enough for that day, and as I led him into the classroom, I hung it on the hook for him. We would save the hanging of the coat for another day.

The following day, the same exercise played out, only for a shorter duration, as it would for the next week, for increasingly shorter durations, followed by an over-the-top expression of praise and gratitude from me, to which he responded most favourably! He began to make eye contact more and more, and would beam, smile and laugh at the end of each successful act of taking off his coat. We had developed a rapport and a connection. I was so glad that I had not given up on that first day, for if I had, all would have been lost. Although I felt like an exorcist at times, it had paid off.

I continued to work with this student for the next three years, including summertime at his home.

I had learned from his response at school during a Friday music session that "The Lion Sleeps Tonight" was one of his favourite songs, and so I programmed three different versions into my cellphone and would play them for him as we walked through the park together. This was a very effective tool for redirecting him when he became agitated. I would continue to use it throughout the course of our association. If I didn't have my phone, I would sing to him, which he seemed to appreciate even more, and which was always met with a warm, knowing smile and laughter.

He quickly became one of my favourite students. I learned to recognize the subtleties of his actions and expressions, and although there were still moments of acting out, I was able to discern quite easily what was genuine angst and what was not. I spoke to him like any other child, and never down to him. I let him know that I understood and respected him, and I know he received it.

There would be the occasional off day, just as we all have, when he would revert back to old ways, but it became a standing joke between us. I would imitate and mirror his behaviour, causing him to turn away and cover his smile, trying to shield from me that he knew I was onto him. He would often burst out into laughter.

I was able to move beyond the surface judgments I had originally made and instead was ultimately able to look deep into this individual and recognize him for who he really is.

I realize that he has taught me just as much, or more, than I have taught him.

As the school year comes to a close and I look toward his graduation, I feel privileged to have had the opportunity to make this connection, and I will greatly miss him. It is with bittersweet joy, sadness and a sense of accomplishment that I say goodbye. I hope that the lessons we have shared together will help pave the way for his future as he soldiers on his journey through life.

Goodbye my friend, best of luck, and most of all, THANK YOU.

Student Group Project

Classroom Group Project

CONRAD

BY JAN GRIFFITHS

In the quiet solitude of the Comfort Room, I had the honour of holding my brother Conrad's hand as he took his last breath and left this world. I made a mental note of the time—2:38 a.m., July 30, 2012. He was sixty years old. A wave of inconsolable grief swept over me.

It was then, in that frozen moment of time, that I began my reflections on Conrad's life.

Conrad was born on May 2, 1952. He was the first of five children born to my parents, Jim and Isobel. It wasn't until Conrad was six months old that they had a diagnosis of "mongolism" or "mental retardation" (medical terms used in that era). We now know it as Down Syndrome.

Many well-meaning doctors recommended that parents place their "mongoloid" children in an institution. They would be a burden, especially if there were siblings. They were "untrainable." But my parents, in their wisdom, welcomed Conrad unconditionally into their hearts and lives.

Conrad became the central figure in our family. Not because he required special care. On the contrary, he was happy, funny, and loved his life and family. And we loved him. As kids, we played for hours outside in our neighbourhood. Dad built a climber/swing set and a sandbox in the back yard. It became a gathering place for lots of friends to play. My mother would introduce Conrad to the neighbourhood kids. She told them that his brain didn't work the same as theirs but that he would like to play with them. At a young age we learned how to negotiate with Conrad and help him to resolve conflict.

We would often ride our bikes up and down the sidewalk. My parents didn't feel that Conrad could manage a bike safely so close to the road, with children all around. So my dad built Conrad a go-cart with peddles. He could keep up with us. He became the envy of all the kids. Conrad felt like a big shot. We were never "made" to play with Conrad. We liked to include him and we sure watched out for him.

When I was ten, I remember visiting a new friend's house for the first time. I asked her where her "retarded" brother was. She said, "I have a brother. He's really annoying but he's not retarded." It just seemed so natural to me to have Conrad in our family. I thought that everyone should have a special brother too!

Conrad went to a special school up until his early teens. He enjoyed going to school with his friends. He participated in all the activities. Conrad learned to print the alphabet and do basic math. He took swimming lessons and entered the Special Olympics. He did well at school. It was a place where he felt valued and smart. As usual, school for Conrad was just another stage for him to perform.

When Conrad was fourteen years old, my mother taught him how to go down to the corner store by himself. She knew that he needed to feel independent. He didn't have to cross any streets. Conrad would proudly take his quarter and buy a pop and ice cream. The storekeeper knew our family and was very friendly. One time when Conrad was making his way to the store, for his adventure he took a rubber ball with him. At the intersection where the store was located, he dropped the ball. It rolled onto the street. A well-meaning lady in her stopped car motioned to Conrad to get the ball. But a truck coming around the corner didn't see him and hit him. The storekeeper called my mom and Conrad was immediately taken by ambulance to the hospital. Conrad suffered a broken leg and superficial head injuries. I remember how incredibly hard it was to see him when he got home. Conrad had a big wound on his forehead and he was crying because he was so scared and it hurt. I felt like I had let him down. I should have been with him. It should've never happened. I couldn't stop crying. It was the first time that I saw Conrad as somewhat fragile. I vowed then to never let it happen again.

In his adult years, Conrad worked at Hutton House in London, Ontario. There he learned how to weave and make pottery. He became proficient at both, mainly because he was a perfectionist. They could always count on him to do the task right. He took pride in his work and was certainly happy, joking with his peers. Once again he felt valued by the staff at Hutton House.

When he was at home, Conrad's favourite pastime was hooking rugs. He would sit for hours, blending colours and announcing who would receive his next creation. Each rug was unique. Anyone who had the honour of receiving one of his treasures still values them as a gift from Conrad's heart.

As a large family, we had many celebrations over the years. Between birthdays, Christmas, weddings, and then babies, we had a lot to be thankful for. Conrad was always the centre of attention. He loved to party. He collected pictures of brides and grooms and even had his own tuxedo. Conrad would dance for hours whenever he was given the opportunity. At my son's wedding, after dancing for hours, he was "last man standing." I said to him, "Connie, move your feet!" He replied, "I can't!" as he looked down at his fancy wedding shoes.

Whenever new babies were born into our family, Conrad would tenderly cradle them. He would whisper to them softly, nuzzle and kiss them lovingly. He always carried pictures of his family with him. If you had the pleasure of talking to Conrad, he would produce the album and proudly share it with you.

When my grandchildren visited Conrad, they would sit with him and colour with him. He loved their company. He was gentle and tender. He would tell them they could keep their pictures. Sometimes he would give them one of his treasured colouring books. I was always impressed with Conrad's ability to endear himself to the little ones.

When Conrad was in his late fifites and declining because of Alzheimer's, I bought him twin dolls. He loved them. They were very real to him. They never left his side and gave him great comfort in his last years.

My parents took care of Conrad his whole life. Due to their physical limitations, my father's debilitating stroke nine years ago and my mother's Alzheimer's, Conrad, my father and my mother all became residents in the same nursing home. Conrad soon endeared himself to the staff who cared for him.

After Conrad's funeral I was going through some boxes at my mother's apartment. I came across all our baby books. I read through Conrad's baby book. Being Mom's first child, she had more time to record his milestones, achievements and funny anecdotes. She recorded his first tooth, first solid food, first steps, first haircut, his favourite foods, books and toys. What impressed me most was that she never once mentioned Conrad's diagnosis! Not once!

My parents raised all of us with respect and love for each other; they didn't tell us to be inclusive, we just did it. This attitude reached beyond

Conrad's sisters and brother to extend to our partners, children and now our grandchildren. What a legacy.

My life's work with children with special needs was a natural progression from what I learned in my family. Conrad taught me about life. Conrad taught me to accept and value those with special abilities…to be patient and experience the miracle of their joy and love. Not to see someone by their "syndrome" or "diagnosis" but rather by their personality, preferences, abilities, and most of all, their heart. And Conrad's heart was incredibly big.

Tile Project

ASMA

BY JANET LEWIS

I wake up, head pounding, ears ringing. It's three-thirty a.m. I think to myself, "Dear God, why would I go in, it's a professional activity day? The students will be at homes. I can stay here at my home if I need to."

In my mind's eye, I think of Alana, the principal, handing out popsicles to children at the school BBQ last night. The thought makes me smile, thinking of how this woman circulates, and keeps us circulating.

I arrive at the school and see the note Alana wrote on the school bulletin board: "Thank you to all the staff who made the BBQ a success. Seeing all the smiles of the children and families who attended is a reflection of your hard work and dedication."

I think of Maddie and Asma, two of the students I work with, who have significant physical impairments.

I recall a moment I shared with Asma this week.

Asma is coiled up in a bean bag chair. I touch her arm and say, "Hi girlie, it's me, Janet." She doesn't move.

"Okay, let's bring your lavender over," I tell her, and bring over the container filled with small purple flowers.

I bring it to her hands, place it between her fingers, let her feel its texture. I bring it up closer to her face and nose. Her nostrils twitch. I keep it under her nose a few seconds longer. She breathes in its scent. She sighs. Then her whole body sighs.

"A morning just turned into a good morning," I whisper to her.

Classroom Project

MADDIE

BY JANET LEWIS

It's a typical day for Maddie. Her usual belly-digestion pain begins shortly after lunch. I give her a bit of warm water to drink. "It's time for the washroom," I tell her. I help her to her feet, bracing her body from behind, and encourage her to take steps forward independently.

As we turn the corner into the washroom, she brushes by the curtains, grasps them tightly, bracing her own self, and pushes her bottom out, bumping me away. She giggles and swings the curtains near me. I gently redirect the curtains back to where they were. "It's time to walk to the toilet, Maddie," I say. She grasps the curtains again and pushes her bottom out. I see the side of her cheeks as she smiles, waiting to see what I'll do.

I smile. I realize she's found a way to delay her trip to the toilet. Given her giggling, she also discovered another way to play, and to tease me a little.

After she sits on the toilet, I help her to her feet, and we shuffle toward the sink. She tries to navigate her feet back toward the curtains. I block her and she pushes her bottom out and vocalizes her objection to my getting in her way.

After washing Maddie's hands, we step together towards the classroom. I let her grasp the curtains one more time. This was not just any trip to the washroom. This time, Maddie taught herself a new way of interacting.

Jake

JAKE AND ME

BY JANINE DENNEY-LIGHTFOOT

My beautiful son, Jake, is autistic. He is funny, playful, sweet and affectionate, mischievous, imaginative and smart as a whip. He remembers everything he hears and never lets me get away with anything. To me, he is perfect. He can be aggressive, which is a big challenge but, otherwise, I think his autism makes him the special and unique little guy that he is. We have some serious challenges and every time I think there's a solution, he gets one step ahead of me, but he is healthy (although he does suffer from anxiety), happy, verbal and completely oblivious to the fact that there's even such a thing as autism. I am hopeful he will go through life blissfully unaware of the fact that he is in any way "different" from others and that he won't know anything about all the conflict and suffering in the world. He can simply live in the moment.

I also suffer from a disability—an invisible one. I was diagnosed as suffering from depression and anxiety when I was a teenager, and it's the kind that will stay with me all of my life. It is generally well-managed with medication but about every eight to ten years I go through a severe episode. My official diagnosis is "very severe refractory depression" (plus anxiety), which means that it doesn't respond well to treatment. I was told early on that I will have severe episodes throughout my life, that each will be worse, last longer and be harder to treat. It was not a prognosis that made me feel better.

Happily, I am enough of an optimist to hope that by the time the next bad episode hits, there will be better medication or better treatments. I've always been advised that I need to live a quiet, stress-free life. But I have ignored that advice completely and choose to live my life in the same way I would if I didn't suffer from depression.

When I was in the midst of my second bad episode, I saw a psychiatrist who I didn't really get along with, but he had suffered from severe depression as well and could really identify with his patients, so I stayed with him. I recall once having a conversation about children. I didn't think I should have children because I was afraid of passing my depression and anxiety on to them and didn't wish that on anyone. I remember suggesting that I might consider adoption but was worried that a children's aid society would refuse to adopt to me because of my mental health issues. And my doctor said that they would probably be right. I've never forgotten how I felt when he said that—it was like telling me that I couldn't possibly be a good parent. And so I gave up on the idea of having children.

But, years later, my "biological clock" began to tick very, very loudly and I became determined to have a child. Then episode three of severe depression set in and it took me three long years to recover. By then, my age was becoming an issue, but I got pregnant.

There was some worry about my medications and I was assessed by the great program at Sick Kids Hospital called MotherRisk, and referred to a specialist who helped me to manage my medication during my pregnancy as I was considered very high risk for postpartum depression.

Jake was born and he changed my life. I sailed through the months after his birth without a hint of depression and for several years I believed that pregnancy had somehow cured my depression (hormonal changes?). Jake brought joy and love into my life like I had never known and he accepted me just the way I am. And through Jake, I have met the most wonderful people. People who are caring, who offer support, who accept and embrace everyone as he or she is—something I had never experienced before.

I have always hidden my depression as best as I could and I have become a fine actress. But when things were bad, I withdrew from the world, and the world let me go. No one ever really tried to help me; I was always the person others came to for help and they didn't realize the extra strain that caused. But the people Jake has brought into my life are fundamentally different. They view life and people differently. They offer me real support when I need it and I know I can reach out to them when I'm really in trouble, something I would never have done in the past.

Though having Jake did not cure my depression—I'm now over three years into episode four and have just completed a new kind of treatment and am finally starting to feel better—he has helped me to focus, and I know I have someone special to live for. I know that no matter what personal demons I have to battle, Jake needs me and I need to be here for him. It doesn't make it easier but it keeps me going.

Jake's autism has helped make him the special child that he is and I wonder sometimes if my depression has given me some good characteristics, like patience and tolerance and acceptance of others. Having Jake, with his disability, has helped bring me to terms with my own disability and to accept myself as I am. Jake's disability and the insight it has given me has probably saved me from mine.

Jennifer Mayr   "Intervention"

THOUGHTS FROM AN INTERVENOR

BY JENNIFER MAYR

T'is true their eyes, they cannot see
And with their ears they cannot hear
But with our hands and belief in them
We can help their words become clear

The road they walk is the same as ours
With many challenges along the way
And for what we use our eyes and ears
They use their hands to say

Their message is the same as ours
Please treat them with respect
And accept their unique disability
And of their differences do not reject

They may be different in how they hear
They may be different in how they see
But they are people with feelings and dreams
Much the same as you and me

Group Project

NEIL

BY JENNIFER ABELL

When I first started teaching at Beverley, I taught children with physical and developmental disabilities, all of whom required diaper changing. Many of them were still tiny and I could lift them myself. All of these children required between one and two hours to feed and change, and so at the end of lunch, one staff member fed the stragglers and the other would change diapers.

On one particular day, most of the students had finished lunch and the current student I was going to change was particularly squirmy on the table. There was no telling how quickly he could move from one end of the change table to the other, and both of my hands and my waist were required to act as an anchor and a barrier to keep him from falling off the table and for changing the diaper.

The method of choice for changing Neil would start by lifting him onto the table. I would put my left hand on his chest and shoulder to calm him and use my right hand to change his diaper. Usually this method seemed to work well, unless we discovered another treasure in the diaper. Bowel movements required a little more speed as Neil would urinate within thirty seconds if the diaper was left off.

The change that day was going fairly well until the discovery and cleaning of Neil's bowel movement. After about the thirtieth second with the diaper off, the anticipated fountain began and I thought I was ready. Neil's body was in the middle of the change table, my left hand on his shoulder and my waist blocking any possible exit. I flipped open the new diaper and tried to position it in a way that I could lift and push the diaper under his bum.

I suppose it would have been prudent to remain calm, staying in the same position until the peeing stopped, but I went into quick action mode trying to make a grab for the dry diaper, which quickly became very wet. The table had a thin film of urine spread on it which enabled Neil a great deal more versatility and movement. As he worked his way down the table he continued to pee, and at that point liquid was spilling over the table onto the floor below. I was slipping on urine, trying to catch Neil before he fell off the table and trying to stem the flow, all at once. A good part of my clothes were soaked, the diaper was soaked, Neil was soaked and ready to fall off the change table. I shrieked and called for help.

A staff member from the adjoining classroom came to assist. She laughed and chortled at the puddle on the floor, my wet shirt and overalls, and Neil's continued attempts to try and stand up.

We did manage to clean Neil, set the bathroom to rights and clean the table, but I smelled like pee for the rest of the day.

Tile Project (Complete)

Group Painting Project

AUTISM IN THE AZORES: A DIARY OF AUTISM, CULTURAL EXPERIENCE AND ACCEPTANCE

BY JENNIFER THOMPSON FERREIRA

My name is Jennifer and my children have special needs. Both my daughter, Lexie, and my son, Nicolas, have autism. I have not written this story to vent or complain to anyone. I have written it to share a story of hope and optimism and love.

Our first year of struggles and challenges was 2005. At three and a half years old, Lexie was diagnosed with high-functioning autism, a speech delay and a cognitive delay. While the developmental assessment was being done on Lexie, baby Nicolas began showing signs of his own trauma—seizures. We had suspected that he was having convulsions for several months, but when he began losing milestones at age one, we finally were able to have him diagnosed at Sick Kids Hospital. Right after Lexie's diagnosis, Nicolas was diagnosed with late onset infantile spasms (baby epilepsy), autism and global developmental delay.

Our family spent several weeks in a tailspin. The adults cried, vented, and melted down. The person who stayed the strongest and never wavered was my sister-in-law, Chris, who gave up work to help me take the kids to doctors' appointments and therapies. Her practical, optimistic attitude helped us get through the first few months. As Chris told the neurologist at Sick Kids, "Well, the diagnosis is what it is, but what are we going to do to make things better? Medication is fine, but we need to get this family sleeping again. Then we can deal with the other problems."

By the spring of that year, my husband, Humberto, and I were struggling with the newness of it all—the medications, the therapies, the never-ending hospital appointments and the concept that both of our children had these problems. I do not remember which family member came up with the idea of the four of us taking a vacation, as a family, to the Azores, Portugal, that summer.

My in-laws, Humberto Sr. and Lourdes, have a small house on the island of Sao Miguel, Azores, an archipelago located in the middle of the Atlantic Ocean, off the coast of Portugal. It is the island of my father-in-law's birth and they have owned a house there since 1991. My first trip was for Christmas 1995. I had spent five vacations in the Azores before autism came into our lives. I loved it so much that my husband and I even had our honeymoon there in 1999. We took Lexie at age one in the summer of 2002, but after the kids' diagnoses, and with their multitude of issues, travel seemed unachievable.

We spent a couple of weeks debating the idea of travel. Our friend Jason, who is Nicolas' godfather, helped us sort things out. He encouraged us to try, and that it just might make us happy. Chris encouraged us to take the trip as well. My parents, Gay and Stan, strongly supported the idea of us going to the Azores.

I was very unsure about travelling so far from home with my son's severe seizures and my daughter's autistic meltdowns. How could this work?

My in-laws were very supportive from the start and we booked a four-week vacation to Sao Miguel to be there with them. It had been three years since I had been. I wanted to go. I wanted to try this but I was nervous and had reservations and doubts about the trip once it was booked. How would we handle a long, overnight, transatlantic flight with our kids? Would it be too stressful taking them out in public in Portugal? Would people be understanding about our situation? Even I had never been to Portugal for such a length of time. Would it be a disaster? What were we thinking?!

I was even more nervous when we boarded because Nicolas was lethargic and had a fever all day. In addition to being ill, his seizures had started again two days before we left, which was devastating after three seizure-free months. Nicolas sat on my lap during the flight because he was still under age two, and Lexie had her own seat. The flight went surprisingly well. Both kids slept on and off. There was one brief, panicky time for us when both kids started crying at the same time, but we got through it.

When we landed in Sao Miguel, I felt like we had just climbed Mount Everest. We had taken our kids on an overnight international flight! I had no idea then what the next four weeks would bring, but when we saw my in-laws waiting for us at the airport, I had hope.

The weather was wonderful. My in-laws' house is located seaside on the beach in Santa Cruz, Lagoa, and Lexie and Nicolas loved the beach. Lexie loved playing in the sand and swimming while Nicolas enjoyed walking along the shore. There is something so wonderfully therapeutic about the Azorean Sea. Some parts of the island have calm ocean and some have rougher ocean. Two things remain the same—the fresh ocean air and the high, beautiful cliffs overlooking the sea. It is a very relaxing atmosphere and it was wonderful to fall asleep with the lull of the ocean waves. The four of us slept well for the first time in months.

Lexie made two friends that summer, Lucia and Andre, who live next door to my in-laws. They befriended Lexie and came over to play with her almost every evening. The language barrier did not even seem to exist, and they all played well together. I wondered if Lucia and Andre knew about Lexie's quirks, but they respected and treated her well. The children also took to Nicolas and tried to play with him as well. At age ten, Lucia explained to my mother-in-law that she knew all about autism and its characteristics. Lucia also told us that Nicolas' behaviors were common for an autistic child.

One afternoon, our other next door neighbor, Maura, visited the house. I did not know Maura well at the time but I liked her. She and her family have become our good friends. Suddenly, Nicolas began having a seizure and we held him, timed the seizure, comforted him, and made sure he was safe. After it was over, Maura looked at us calmly and told my mother-in-law that she knew it was a seizure right from the beginning, and asked if Nicolas was okay. There was no staring, no judgment, no strange looks, no panicking. Just acceptance.

By the spring of 2006, we had survived almost one year of commuting across Toronto to a special needs preschool, months of speech and occupational therapies, school struggles for Lexie who was now in junior kindergarten, Nicolas' horrible seizures—all amidst one wonderful miracle, the birth of my niece, Vicki, to my sister-in-law Chris and her husband Ric.

By that summer, Humberto and I decided we needed a getaway. We would, again, take the kids back to Sao Miguel. The flight was quiet and uneventful. When we walked through the airport terminal in Sao Miguel, I felt like I had returned home.

Within two days of our arrival, Nicolas' seizures stopped after starting a new medication. We suddenly had a vibrant, energetic, alert, playful two-and-a-half-year-old boy on our hands. That summer, Nicolas hugged us for the first time ever. We had waited almost three years for that moment! How wonderful that it happened in Portugal.

Humberto and I both knew we needed and wanted to return to Sao Miguel in 2007. We were becoming more tired and stressed from our kids' needs as each year passed. We booked a three-week trip in August. This time, however, our flight was quite stressful.

The plane ride was smooth and the service was good, but Nicolas was stressed and upset and he screamed for the entire five-hour flight. We took turns holding him, comforting him and walking him up and down the aisle. Nothing seemed to work.

A nearby passenger with two older kids offered us some candy to help clear Nicolas' ears. I thanked him and told him that Nicolas was autistic and could not eat hard candy. After that, other people on the flight approached us and patted Nicolas' head and stroked his back, reassuring both of us at the same time. Not one person gave us a dirty look or complained. Everyone was sympathetic. They understood. This little boy was in distress. We could not stop it. It was beyond our control. The Portuguese culture adores and appreciates children (as it should be) and that was evident on this flight.

Lexie really blossomed that summer. She and her grandfather frequently walked up the street to the Igreja de Santa Cruz, the local church. Lexie has a big interest in Catholicism, and these were great bonding moments for them. Lexie also improved her swimming skills, and my husband Humberto and I were able to take her on dates, just the three of us. It made Lexie very happy to have alone time with us.

We survived quite a roller-coaster ride in 2008 with Lexie. That year, at age seven, she was diagnosed with ADD, LD, anxiety and depression. Lexie is an intelligent girl and very sensitive. She could not differentiate between her autism and her brother's autism, and therefore developed anxiety over having the same diagnosis. By the summer of 2009, things had improved for her quite a bit. We were ready for a break. We planned another trip to Sao Miguel. We were very excited after a two-year absence. My in-laws were booked, we were booked, and surprise—my parents were booked! They had never been to Portugal and we arranged for them to stay in a pensao residencial (bed and breakfast) for one week while we were all there. A great time was had by all.

Wherever we went that summer, people smiled at us, were friendly, and accepted us. No one gave us funny looks and no one made us feel self-conscious. Nicolas was very loud. While still nonverbal, he stimmed—murmured and hummed—loudly. His favourite expression was "in-gee," which he would call out as he stood at the foot of the ocean, flapping his arms.

That summer, Nicolas and I walked all over the village. We frequently walked to the church, the town square and to the soccer pitch to watch games. One evening, we were walking on the Avenida in front of the house and one of the neighbours passed by. She saw how Nicolas had grown and changed, and stopped to play with him. He was so engaging with her, hugging her and leading her by the hand to run and jump with him. I do not speak very much Portuguese and she spoke no English, but it did not matter. It was the international language of children and kindness.

We also met Sergio and Suzie that summer. Sergio is the brother of our next-door neighbour, Ana Maria. Sergio and Suzie were visiting from another island, Pico, for a couple of weeks. Their daughter, Erica, is Lexie's age, and they had a great time playing together. It was wonderful to see the two girls playing and using the computer to watch *Hannah Montana* videos. I was so happy to see Lexie content, satisfied and carefree. This trip to Portugal was healing for her. She was able to play, enjoy nature and, more importantly, be herself.

We returned to the Azores in the winter and summer of 2010. In February, we stayed for twelve days and had a great time despite the cold, wind and rain. We took drives, walks and shopped. We were able to see the festivities for Carnival (Mardi Gras) in Ponta Delgada. We all sat on the church steps watching the parade, and a group of special needs adults from a group home came and sat with us. They were all so excited about the music, costumes and streamers. Strangers walking by would stop to shake hands with one of the young men who was verbal, and they hugged and chatted. The amount of caring and compassion from the staff was incredible. These workers were showing the adults a good, fun time, integrating them into community activities.

One day, while Humberto and I walked around Parque Atlantico, the huge shopping centre in Ponta Delgada, we saw a group of medically fragile children being wheeled around the mall in medical beds. We were so happy that the staff for this group were trying to show the kids a good time by taking them for a "walk," in this case, indoors. I have noticed that this concept of inclusion seems so easily accepted in Portugal.

We returned to Sao Miguel again this past summer and had a wonderful time. We also saw a festival in Ribeira Grande, a town on the northern part of the island. I took photographs of special needs groups performing dances in the procession. It was incredible to see such efforts at inclusion and acceptance. Another example of this is the fact that even Nicolas has made friends with the pool lifeguards at Caloura, where there is a beautiful salt-water pool. The lifeguards see Nicolas there regularly and have come to know him over the last couple of summers. They always make it a point to talk to him, touch his hands and speak English words to him. They also appreciate how much Nicolas loves the water and love to watch his enjoyment.

A highlight of this trip was attending Maura and Luis Miguel's wedding. We haven't attended, or been invited for that matter, to too many weddings, so this was very special. We made the effort to book our flights around the wedding date. It was wonderful to walk up the hill to the church with the bride and her family. We drove our cars in a wedding procession through the village after the ceremony. It was so much fun! At the reception, we sat at the table with Luis' cousin Saul and his family, who are also from Toronto. Lexie chatted with Saul's daughter Britney and they got along well.

Unfortunately, Nicolas was having a bad night and had crying fits. Everyone was very understanding, though, and we still had fun. Nicolas played on the iPad with Leticia, Luis' niece, who is seven years old and also autistic. Leticia is high functioning and she and Nicolas seem to have a peaceful, accepting relationship. They enjoy each other's company. Luis, who could see that Lexie was having a great time, offered to drive her home later if we needed to get Nicolas home early.

Before we arrived in Sao Miguel this summer, staff at the local grocery store, Modelo, had been asking my in-laws about Nicolas. They were wondering if we were coming to the island and made sure to emphasize that they wanted to see Nicolas when we arrived. I guess many people on the island have been watching Nicolas grow up and come of age, as we are watching their kids do the same.

My children both love the Azores. My husband and I love the Azores. I have spent many years talking about the islands to friends, family, neighbours and coworkers. The island of Sao Miguel has been amazing for my family and it is a legacy I am proud to pass on to my kids. It is a legacy we would pass on whether autism was in our lives or not. Since autism is in our lives, we accept it and enjoy our years with autism in the Azores.

Group Project

BEING A FAMILY

BY JORDAN CLELAND

Rain can make or break your day. Especially when your day consists of sitting in a large piece of wood and using another piece of wood and just your arm strength to travel. That first piece of wood being, of course, a canoe and the second, a paddle. The lake we were on was so immense that not only could you look up and see the cloud that was raining on you, but you could also see ahead of you to where the rain stopped. It gave you the smallest amount of futile hope that, if you could just paddle fast or strong enough, you could get out from the miserable sprinkling.

The day hadn't been very successful—we were late getting onto the water and as soon as we had started to get into the swing of things it had started to rain. With every droplet that rolled off my rain jacket, my mood worsened until I haphazardly threw a glance over at my youngest brother and suddenly a laugh bubbled up inside me. He had his face turned towards the sky, and a smile so big it could swallow all the rain, clouds and misery. With every drop that hit his face, he would blink rapidly to clear his eyes, but, with every drop that hit his face, his smile grew.

When Nigel was born, we had no idea. He developed fine until, way after the age that most babies can sit on their own, he simply could not. My parents were worried but they waited it out. But one by one other milestones were not met and after many tests, the truth surfaced: Nigel had a severe developmental disability. While we grappled with this fact, trying to understand it, and trying to accept it, Nigel had a seizure while he was sleeping and was rushed to the hospital. Thanks to a plethora of tests, the doctors discovered that he also was epileptic. The next few years were a blur of overnight stays at the hospital, seizures, tears and confusion. Nigel's seizures started to become a part of our normal routine, but they scared me.

The seizures would have varying degrees of intensity—sometimes he would get a blank look and his hand would twitch and sometimes his eyes would roll back in his head, his body would become rigid and he would surrender the rights of his body to his malfunctioning brain. I could deal with his seizures but I preferred not to—leaving the room if my parents were there looking after him. It got to the point where I was scared to be alone with him, my own brother, scared of having to deal with something so foreign.

The rain slowly grew stronger and, as the distinct cloud above us blurred into a grey sky, we decided to pull over and wait it out. I dragged my paddle in the water, steering the canoe over to the rocks, the rain droplets seeming to come from below as they splashed up from the lake. My other brother, Theo, climbed quickly out of the canoe and sat on the front of it to steady it. As I was climbing out, my parents' and Nigel's canoe pulled up beside us and scraped onto the rocky shore. Inside, I cringed. It wasn't the most ideal situation when neither of my parents really camped, let alone knew how to steer a canoe.

We all scampered to get out of the canoes, pull them ashore and to dig out the tarp we had in one of our musty, borrowed packs. My father, as usual, busied himself with Nigel—precariously half-sliding, half-lifting him, first to the front of the boat and then out. The rain poured steadily down on us until I finally found the tarp and threw one end to Theo and we pulled it over all of us. Nigel was blinking furiously trying to get all the remaining water out of his eyes.

As we sat under the tarp with rain water dumping down on us, on the now muddy ground, we all had sour expressions on our faces except Nigel who was now in the process of looking around our new shelter and trying to pull it down around us.

"Nigel, stop pulling the tarp," my dad said, taking Nigel's hand and removing it from the wet fabric. His hand, of course, shot back up to the exact spot it was before and continued tugging on the bright blue fabric.

"Nigel, enough."

We could all tell that my dad's patience levels were low—it happened to all of us sometimes and when it did, we would be strict with him as if we thought, or hoped, he could understand. As always, as soon as my dad removed his hand, it shot back up again and latched onto the tarp. So here we were, a miserable, wet bunch squatting under a muddy tarp on the first day of our "adventure" and asking ourselves why we decided to do something like this.

> *During the next few years, Nigel met a whole lot of different kinds of people—physiotherapists, specialists for all kinds of things that I couldn't pronounce, neurologists and everybody in between. He attended weekly appointments with a physiotherapist who tried to help him walk. She would hold his heels and make him step up and down wooden blocks, stand up against the wall and balance on a wooden board. After a few months of therapy, the woman told my parents that my brother would never walk and that she was, after this conversation, no longer available to help such a lost, hopeless cause.*
>
> *Several years later, my brother was walking. My father had seen what the therapist did and had, with endless dedication and overwhelming love, continued Nigel's therapy. To put it plainly, I think that was Nigel's special way of extending a big and overwhelming "f- you" to that woman.*

The reason for Nigel's disability was never diagnosed. His chromosome count is right; everything seems to be in working order on a biological level. Many people who have family members with disabilities see this as an extreme disadvantage because we'll never know its origins or the prognosis. As much as I see it as a drawback, in the end I truly see it as a blessing. Living with my brother's undiagnosed disability has freed my family and the people he meets from stereotyping him. He will never fit into a category, he will always evade labels. He will always defy people's expectations.

On a personal level, I see no need for a diagnosis. Nigel is Nigel—people without disabilities do not get diagnoses, they are not shoved into small categories until they fit and they are not told what they are (or are not). People without disabilities are not told what they can or cannot do. People without disabilities just are. And so is Nigel.

"This is so dumb. I hate this. Fu—" Theo quickly realized that he was about to swear and stifled his sentence. My parents didn't even react—a sure sign that they were in a bad mood. Usually, my mother jumps on slip-ups with a very stern look and a raised eyebrow, which is usually enough to make us apologize profusely for any misdemeanours we commit.

The rain seemed to lighten up for a second and my dad took full opportunity to bring Nigel into the woods to go to the bathroom. As I watched him get up, help Nigel up and slowly help him walk off into the woods, I was reminded about how it will never be easy. My brother is just going to keep growing, and helping him move around will just become harder. I tried not to think about it. To distract myself I started to punch and tickle Theo to try and get him into a better mood. The thought was quickly pushed out of my mind as Theo got annoyed and we started bickering. Nigel and my dad eventually came back and slowly the mood under that tarp reverted back to silent brooding.

The doctors finally got something right: Nigel's medication. His seizures were suppressed while he was awake—the demons were left to torment his body during the night. After Nigel's medication was in the right dosage, all we had to worry about was the daily physical threat he was in because he was not able to control his body.

My family and I took a month-long trip to France in the summer of 2004. Nigel was four years old and the trip went spectacularly. On the last leg of the trip, we found ourselves settled comfortably in a villa in the south of France. Leading from the driveway to the villa there was a beautiful stone staircase that curved at the last two steps. We had returned from an outing and, as usual, Theo and I rushed inside, my mom trailing in after us and my father bringing Nigel out of the car and down the stairs. He placed him into his wheelchair and, as he had done a thousand other times, starting bumping him down the stairs.

In the blink of an eye, my father was left holding only the handles as they detached from the body of the chair. He watched as the chair bounced down the stairs, out of control, with my brother strapped into it. From inside the house, I heard Nigel's scream. The scream that I heard rocked my bones and without even thinking, I flew towards the door, my mother and Theo right beside me. We were greeted by the horrific sight of my dad standing shocked at the top of the stairs and my brother's wheelchair upside down at the bottom, with my precious boy trapped underneath it. What happened after that is a blur, but, with Nigel's screams echoing throughout the house, his wheelchair was righted, he was removed from underneath it and I telephoned the emergency number. A doctor was assigned to come to our villa as soon as possible.

As the panicked, scared note of Nigel's cries dissolved into shaky tears, Nigel began to get sleepy. He was bleeding from his forehead but from what we could see it was only a shallow scratch. When he began to drift off into slumber we got scared and assumed the worst—doing our best to keep him awake because of the fear of a concussion. The amount of pain felt by every person in my family that day in France was unforgettable. A day later, Nigel was fine and smiling again. I thank God, or whoever was watching him that day, that the only thing that he got was a very large scratch and a scare.

We sat under that tarp for what seemed like hours until the rain finally stopped. Stuffing the tarp back into the pack, we tried to dry ourselves out a little bit with no success—at all. Theo stormed off, annoyed, and was just stepping into the canoe, when his foot hit an unusually slippery rock and he went sliding into the lake up to his chest. There was a moment of deathly silence. But then Nigel started laughing. Theo took one glance at him and burst into laughter. With the tension broken, we all laughed so hard we could hardly contain ourselves. They say laughter is the best medicine, and sometimes with my family, I truly believe it is.

Nigel does that sometimes. He laughs at the exact right moment, as if he can understand everything we're saying. And maybe he can.

Life continued as usual. There were some mishaps and sometimes we were scared...but with many laughs and love because of my brother's disability. Every person in my life gravitated towards Nigel, so much so that as I got older I began to judge people on how well they interacted with him. I truly believe that he has a huge impact on many people's lives. He, in the very least, helps people be more accepting towards others. He forces people to look past the wheelchair, the drool and the disability to see the beautiful soul that shines.

We eventually got to the campsite and, after setting everything up, separated to do our own things. I sat around (I do that a lot) and wished I had my cellphone. After a while, I pulled out a notebook and started to write. I find that being in the wilderness with no technological distractions just inspires words to be written on pages. Theo immediately sat down by the water in a "cool-yet-contemplating" pose that he probably mastered before we left—in case any girls were around. He then skipped rocks, yelling occasionally to my mom to watch how far he could throw them just to prove how strong he is. He does that a lot too. My mom made a cup of tea over the stove and began to read. My dad fed Nigel and explored the campsite looking for cool things to show us. When he couldn't find anything, he got out a book and started to read as well. Nigel just sat in his chair, looking around. From the outside, we looked like a completely normal family.

That being said, life is not always smiles and laughs with Nigel's disability. I still remember the day my mother told me that the doctors said he will never talk. She had tears running down her face. It took me years to finally understand the gravity of what she told me. It meant he'll never be able to ask for what he wants. He'll never be able to tell us when he is uncomfortable, when he is happy. He'll never be able to say "I love you."

But as I have grown up alongside my brother, I have come to realize that Nigel doesn't need words as much as we originally thought. Nigel asks for what he wants by looking at it, squealing, pulling us towards it, in any way possible. He says he is uncomfortable by furrowing his brow slightly—a facial expression which every person in my family is finely-tuned to pick up on. He says he's happy by laughing so hard he can't breathe, by hugging us around the neck, by kissing us sometimes (if we're lucky). He says "I love you" simply in the way he looks at you. You can't miss it. Without words, Nigel is more honest than many people I know. If he loves you, you know.

Another thing that we rarely smile and laugh about is the future. I know my parents worry about it. I can see it in them. They worry about where Nigel will live when they pass away. They wish that he could lead a normal life and live on his own. They wish he could find a wife and marry her and have children. My mom and dad have tentatively approached the subject with Theo and I—the subject of "our responsibilities" when they are gone. Their will has been divided to favour Nigel because he will never make his own money. They have told us that neither of us can move too far away from Toronto because Nigel will be our responsibility some day. That was a lot to shoulder a few years ago when they told us. It's a lot to shoulder still. I think it always will be.

Family trips always went a little like this. We did a whole lot of hanging around, occupying ourselves with card games and other little time wasters. And sometimes we just sat. And as much as Theo and I had complained before we left, it was actually nice just to hang out with my family. The trip went on like this for three days. It was sometimes rainy, sometimes sunny. Sometimes hilarious, sometimes boring. Nigel just loved every minute of it. He was, however, a little too excited to be sleeping with us so it took awhile to get him to bed every night.

That was probably the most eventful thing that happened on our canoe trip. Bet you thought something big was going to happen, eh? In the end, I took a few moments to reflect on what I had learned during such an uneventful trip. I realized how well we, as a family, work. Throughout all our hardships, our successes and even through the boring times, we just work. We—knowingly or unknowingly—support each other. We embrace each other for our faults and for our strengths. We love my darling brother for what he is—we do not focus on what he cannot do. Sometimes it's hard to remain positive, because often with disability comes sadness, insecurity and hopelessness. But my family fights back hard against all that. My mom, dad and brother instil hope in me—for the present and for the future.

Their refusal to bend under the weight of it all, their strength, keeps me strong. Every person is ready to do what is necessary for my brother to lead a happy and fulfilling life. My parents have remained a strong unit throughout my whole life. They raised two kids to teenagers, while never once letting Nigel's disability impact negatively on us. They never ignored us. They never brushed us off. Somehow, the two of them found each other and, although they are strong on their own, they are unstoppable together. They didn't sign up for this, but if anybody is capable of pushing this family to the best we can be, it's my parents. I look up to them more than they could ever know. Theo has also been incredibly inspiring to me throughout Nigel's life and our contemplation of the future. He has happily said that he's going to buy a mansion when he's older and give Nigel a whole wing. Theo loves Nigel to his very core. I can just tell. There are no words that could say it better than his actions and body do.

We are not five individuals who happen to live together. We are not five people who haphazardly fell into each other's lives. We are a family. And together we can face anything.

Funny how a little thing like that could have been discovered on a boring canoe trip.

Jennel

TRICKED

BY JULIE GRANT

After one swim period, Lisa, our lifeguard, decided to entertain the students who were waiting for their classmates to be changed. She donned a pair of flippers, an inner tube, a lifejacket, goggles and water wings and proceeded to dance.

Just as Lisa's dance started to pick up steam, a fully clothed student, Eddie, emerged from the change room and lurched toward the pool. As we watched and muttered our futile "no's," Lisa clumsily leapt, encumbered by flippers, across the pool deck and snatched Eddie just as he was about to dive into the pool.

Eddie, knowing he had nearly tricked us, gave us a mischievous sideways smile just before he left.

Beverley Summer School Project

MORE THAN THINGS

BY KEITHA HALSTEAD AND ASMA MEDINA

During my childhood, I had a special blanket that was part of my growing up. It reflected a special part of me that made me feel secure. This blanket came with me wherever I went, although at times my mother didn't know I had it with me. When I didn't have this blanket with me, I felt alone.

Why? I guess it may have been the smell of it combined with my mother, sister and father's scent and also the smell of home.

I felt so at ease knowing that my family would always be with me on my travels with this blanket. The touch, the feel and the colour of it was a big part of my early years. Even at fourteen, I kept this blanket with me when I went to sleep at night.

At Beverley School, I see so many students who have many different objects, toys and sensory items that help them to feel secure and soothe their active senses, and I always think back to my blanket and how important it was to me.

Tile Project

TO THE POINT

BY LAURA JOHNSTON

"Did you see that?" I asked my husband, gesturing towards our son. "See what?" he queried.

"Jasper just pointed!" I replied, my excitement growing. Running over to Jasper, I gave him a hug and saw the object of his point—some goldfish.

So what's remarkable about that, you might ask. Every child points—right? Well, it turns out, not every child does point. A child not pointing by the time they reach one-and-a-half years can be a sign of autism. In our case it is Fragile X with autism.

But let me back up a few years. When our son Jasper wasn't hitting his communication milestones by nine months, I had a gut feeling that something wasn't right. Like every family with a special needs child, our path to a diagnosis was fraught with despair (what is wrong with my child) to hope (he's fine, he's just a late-bloomer) to finally an answer—Fragile X.

Fragile X is the most common inherited form of mental impairment and affects 1 in 4,000 boys and 1 in 6,000 girls. In many cases, people with Fragile X exhibit autistic traits, with as many as twenty-five percent formally receiving the diagnosis of autism.

We received our diagnosis right before Christmas, close to Jasper's second birthday. It was quite the Christmas present—but in some ways, it actually was a present because it gave us something to work with. The answer we craved. Now began our new life P.D. (Post-Diagnosis).

So, back to Jasper's finger point.

A point is just a point, except when it's a point that you never expected to see. With Jasper, all the normal things you'd hope to see with your child never seemed to materialize—like words, waves or points, hugs or kisses. Not a chance. So you'd wipe them off your list of *can't-wait-to-see-it-happen* and put them on your *it-would-be-nice-but-I'm-not-holding-my-breath* list, which you keep in the back of a closet and choose to forget about—hope can be heartbreaking.

That's not to say we didn't have other things to celebrate—like his ability to use pictures, and now an iPad to communicate (huge!), or making it through a grocery store without a complete meltdown (phew!). But you also crave some of those "normal" things that you had hoped to see.

So when things that are on that list, which you keep hidden in the back of that closet, start to reveal themselves—they seem like gifts from heaven above.

That point, that Jasper so beautifully demonstrated, happened when he was about six years old, five years after I thought it would arrive—and it truly was a thing of beauty. And then, at seven, came his first wave hello—and my heart soared. And now, at age eight, he treats me to hugs and if I'm really lucky, a snuggle. I'm almost afraid to breathe when he snuggles in beside me so as not to disturb the moment.

And that is the thing about having a special needs child—the little things in life that you would normally consider insignificant become celebrations filled with fireworks, whoops of joy and phone calls to grandparents, aunts and uncles. Even now, when I see Jasper point or wave I can't help but smile. Those mundane gestures will always be extraordinary to me.

Giorgis

Student Group Project

HELLO, MY NAME IS LEXIE

BY LEXIE FERREIRA

Hello, my name is Lexie Ferreira. I'm eleven years old and in grade six. I go to Leslieville Junior Public School. It is really crowded at my school because at my school we have full day kindergarten at my school and it feels crowded at my classroom. My classroom has thirty-three kids in my class plus me, and I'm a student called an HSP student. I am in two classes—one in the morning and one in the afternoon. It is pretty hard being in my classes because of three things:

A) I sometimes get bullied
B) My teacher in the morning doesn't even know me and
C) I hardly have any friends.

The reason why I hardly have any friends is because I have a small thing called autism. I'm really shy and I get upset really easily and it's really hard for me to get along with people. Like last week this guy called me a weirdo, so I got a little upset and called him a jerk. But afterwords I felt a little bit guilty but I never apologized because he always calls me weirdo but I live with it.

I also feel upset when people are always blurting in my face that they get to go to Senior parties and I'm stuck somewhere when they are having the time of their lives. But hey I live with it just like I sometimes live with bullying. There is this kid and he makes fun of me and says that he is better than me. Well the truth is that no one is better than anyone. He may think that he is better than me but he is actually really sometimes selfish. No one is better than anyone. Like I said I am not PERFECT but I am still good. I may not have like a hundred friends but I have friends that care for me and I care for them too! I don't want anything to happen to them when I am away or when they are away too. The thing is that I have the right amount of friends with me here right now and right here. I never wanted to be bullied or be called names but I live with it.

I am really into reading, writing and drawing. I also like math too. My teacher, Mrs. Jacobs, is the best teacher I ever had and she helps me with my problem and she says I can tell her anything. I told her that I have a small curve in my back called scoliosis and that I think that's why I can not do backflips off the monkey bars and thats why I cannot get out of the pool really well. But I don't care, it's nothing and I don't care if I have scoliosis. I'm not going to let anything stand in my way. It's my life and I can do anything I want to do with my life.

My fave meal is mac & cheese and pizza. I also have a brother named Nicolas. He is nine years old and technically in grade four. My little brother is autistic too. He cannot speak, he can't talk, he can't really do anything, but I still love him and that's what makes him special.

Well thank you for reading my story about my life and my little brother's life too!

(P.S. Sorry for some misunderstood words and for the long story.)

Bye-Bye

Lexie Ferreira
Age eleven and a quarter
Wednesday, November, seventh 2012

Room 117 Collaboration

Group Tile Project

THE BEAMER

BY LYDIA SAI-CHEW

Still, every once in a while, I'll be hit by profound sadness about the Beamer's disability. This weekend it happens as we're doing our usual walk along the retail street in our neighbourhood. The Hubby always asks, "Where to?" but he doesn't have to because he knows. It's always to the other end. To the Starbucks. If the Hubby and I are doing the walk by ourselves, it takes about fifteen minutes each way. But when we go with the Beamer, it's an outing. The Beamer walks part of the way. He doesn't quite understand the point of going in one direction, in a straight line. There are so many interesting things and people to see off to each side and even behind. Many of the store windows have his nose print on it.

On this day, the street fair has brought out all the young families. Strollers and toddlers abound. Cute little kids with painted faces, eating ice cream, marvelling at balloon creations. Some of the kids stare at the Beamer. They know he is one of them, but not one of them. I cast my love protectively around him. I know it's irrational and completely misplaced but I feel resentment at all the happy-looking families with their beautiful, perfect-looking children. The Hubby and I are pushing our stroller too. But instead of a perfect toddler, we are pushing our beautiful, imperfect twelve-year-old. I turn down the offer of a balloon. What's the point? The Beamer would not even notice it. We rush by face painting. The Beamer would never sit still for its application. A freezie is declined. The Beamer would not know what to do with it.

Then, almost to the Starbucks, a woman who I have never seen before speaks to me. She is compelled to tell me that she often notices the Beamer when he's on one of our walks because he always gives her the most amazing smile. I thank her. And I feel a little better. Then I remember that at the beginning of our walk a man had passed us, and as he did, he turned to look at me and gave me a very familiar smile. I asked the Hubby, "Who was that?" The Hubby had no idea. A little while later, a woman with a little dog came out of a store as we were passing and she also gave me a huge smile. The Hubby asked, "Who was that?" I had no idea. This happens regularly when we walk with the Beamer. People we don't know, know the Beamer. The Beamer smiles at them. They smile at the Beamer. Then they smile at us. And I smile to myself.

Group Project

Majeed

LESSONS FROM THE BEAMER

BY LYDIA SAI-CHEW

It's the Beamer's birthday. For the past twelve years I've been trying to learn what my son is trying to teach me. This is what I've figured out so far.

1. Approach each day with delight. Greet everyone with a smile and an open heart. With this you will attract kind, generous, good people. As soon as the Beamer wakes up in the morning, he's smiling. Like he can't believe his good fortune. Like he expects only good things to be waiting for him. A trip to the grocery store isn't a boring chore. It's an opportunity to check out the goods in other people's carts, try raw potatoes and bananas with their skins on, eye the oh-so-interesting bottles and jars on the shelves.

2. Be present in the moment. This way you get the full experience of whatever you're doing and you don't miss any good stuff by being preoccupied with other stuff. Like when the Beamer has a bath. I know he is savouring every wonderful second in the tub. The water is lovely and warm. The bath toys are beyond expectation. You never know when someone's going to pull the plug.

3. When someone does something mean it might not be because the person is rude or doesn't like me or is angry. It could be that this person just really wants my attention and can't figure out a better way to get it. Scarlett, the Beamer's eight-year-old cousin, suggests that this is what's going on when the Beamer pulls her hair.

4. Talk less. Say more. The Beamer doesn't talk. But when his brow gets a little furrow in it we all know that something is causing him consternation: I need you. A sparkle in his eyes: I love you. Hone it down to the essentials. That's all you really need to get by.

The Daughter made a surprise visit home from university for the weekend to celebrate her brother's birthday. We all knew what he was thinking when he wrapped his arms around her head and went cheek to cheek: Ahhh...there you are! I was wondering where you'd been?! All is now right in the world.

Happy Birthday, sweet boy.

Tile Project

Classroom Project

JOHNNIE'S POEM

BY MADELEINE STANDISH

If only I had realized I was a day too late,
Spending my time seeing only omens
And death, while we waited for the end.

I was an hour too late to realize the untamed flames from his head
Were dulling the devil in his brain that had finally ceased.
Finally he was peaced.

I was a minute too late with sun rays in through the window.
He lay unmoving, no omen or dark cloud hovering above my family.
He was an angel and I only realized a second too late.

Classroom Collaboration

CONCHI'S BUS

BY MARIA GUERRA DECASTRO

It's a cold Tuesday morning in Toronto. I unlock the door to my bus. Like every day, I make eight stops to bring eight children to Clinton Public School for their daily programming in a special needs classroom.

When the parents help their children onto the bus, they kiss them goodbye, they hug, they wave and wish them a good day. They are glad that their children are learning important skills at school. They are glad to know their children are well looked after so they can do the work they need.

I say "hello" and "happy to see you" to each one as they settle into their green vinyl seats.

I've been a driver for almost twelve years. Some of the students I've taken to school for eight years. When they first got on my bus, they were nervous. They looked scared. For them, I was a new face. The older ones know they are going to school. They are used to the routine. But the little ones are confused and scared because at the beginning, they don't know where I'm taking them. They are nonverbal, and even though myself and the parents have reassured them, school and a school bus is still a new idea.

If I take a different route, the routine is broken, and that can be scary, especially for a child who doesn't communicate verbally. But I know changes in the route can scare them because they cry, or kick, or I can see it on their faces when I peek in my overhead mirror.

When I first started, it was difficult for me to read their feelings. Each of them, in their own special way, are in their own world. They rock in their chairs. They hum. There are happy hums and anxious hums. To start, they all stay pretty silent, keeping to themselves, staring out the window, doing the things they need to stay comfortable.

Each day, in the morning and afternoon, I take every opportunity to talk to them, even though they have never spoken words to me. Every time I stop, for a traffic light, stop signs, intersections, in traffic, I call out to them, ask them questions, even though they don't respond, ask them about their day, tell them good things and happy thoughts.

One day, I decided to bring in my CDs to play for the kids. Once I had made all my stops, and my small yellow bus was filled, I pressed Play. The choral singing, the Spanish guitar, the drums, filled the air of the bus. The children couldn't understand the lyrics, but they felt the joy. Their response was exuberant. Their eyes lit up. They tapped to the beat. They hummed along. They even learned some words in Spanish. Some closed their eyes as they felt the impact of what they were hearing. There was something in the music, in the air, that moved them and enriched their thirty-minute ride to school.

For me, this was an accomplishment. I was so happy to see how the kids progressed, how they responded to music and interaction. They loved the attention; they loved the acknowledgement. Even though they didn't show the usual signs of listening, they were.

I love my job as a bus driver, and the kids love to be on my bus. I feel so lucky to be part of their lives.

Tile Project

Classroom Collaboration

MY GREATEST TEACHER

BY MICHAEL-JAMES PALAZZO

As we become more conscious of the uniqueness of others, we become aware of our common humanity.

- Jean Vanier

The greatest teachers in my life have been individuals who are often referred to as "marginalized" and are frequently "othered" in our society. I have been fortunate to form meaningful relationships with physically and mentally exceptional individuals throughout the course of my life. When I think back to the memories I share with such individuals and consider the immensely substantive effect that they have had on me as both an individual and as an educator, I feel an overwhelming sense of gratitude for the love and respect that they have gifted to me.

Various significant life experiences have informed my calling to become a teacher and educator of diverse learners. One such life experience was that of growing up with an uncle who had severe physical and intellectual exceptionalities. At the age of eight he was diagnosed with polyarteritis nodosa, a disease of unknown cause that destroys blood vessels due to hyper inflammation of the arteries. He experienced his first stroke at the age of twelve and spent most of his life in and out of hospital rooms. My uncle taught me about vulnerability, patience, and unconditional love. He taught me a new lesson about life each day that I spent with him. I learned how to be grateful for the many gifts and blessings in my life and to honour those idiosyncratic moments that we often overlook and take for granted. My relationship with my uncle and his overall life legacy led me to develop an enhanced sensitivity to the needs and gifts of particularly vulnerable children.

In forming a significant relationship with my uncle at an early age I was able to lift a veil of misunderstanding and ignorance that had been gradually placed over my eyes as a result of the constant bombardment of information coming from media and popular culture that depict individuals with exceptionalities as "less than" or not able to function effectively in our society. In school, I was always sensitive to the needs of my classmates no matter the exceptionality that they were learning to live with in their early lives.

Another enriching moment in my life transpired throughout the course of time I spent at L'Arche in Trosly, France. Founded by Jean Vanier, the son of former Governor General Georges Vanier, L'Arche is an international organization that has created homes and support networks for individuals who are physically and intellectually exceptional. My greatest teacher within this particular L'Arche community was a middle-aged woman who was deaf, blind and completely paralyzed from the neck down. When we went together for strolls through the park, she would not be able to contain her joy and love for the outdoors. She was able to appreciate the beauty of nature simply by feeling cool air on her face or by inhaling the aroma of freshly bloomed flowers in a garden. I marvelled at the self-transformation I felt after spending time with Jean Vanier and the community in Trosly, in the wake of experiencing such a strong sense of community and togetherness grounded in love and respect for diversity and difference.

Perhaps my most "life" significant experience working with young people with diverse learning needs, took place throughout my time as a student teacher at Beverley Public School. I often consider Beverley to be a L'Arche community for young people, as the staff are representative of a family unit who completely devote themselves to their student community. Throughout my time at Beverley, students taught me what it means to genuinely engage and actively listen to one another. They showed me that one's truest opinions and emotions can be well articulated without having to speak verbally. They taught me what it means to be fully human. They are the reason why I am an educator.

Eyob

WHO WE ARE

BY NICKI CAMPBELL

I am an angel. I am a saint. I am full of patience. These are all things I have been told by strangers while on trips or walks with my students. For a long time, I could not figure out why these comments, or intended compliments, bothered me so much. I hope this helps to explain my frustration. These assumptions about who, and what, I am are based on assumptions about who, and what, my students are. Those strangers have all believed several things about my students. They are helpless. They are incapable of emotions. They can't learn. This must be a group home trip because children like this don't go to school (yes, I have been asked this several times while in the community). I constantly find myself getting upset with the community for not being informed of what it means for people to live with disabilities, so I hope this offers a bit of education.

Assumptions about me:

Angel/Saint. Let me set the record straight—I am no angel. I wake my kindergarten students up if they arrive sleeping on the bus, I make them wear their orthotics for the recommended amount of time, and I probably push them harder than they have ever been pushed in their lives. While doing so, I encourage, I motivate, I congratulate, and I celebrate. When we go on trips and able-bodied people try to sneak into the elevator before us instead of taking the escalator, I find the fight rising from within me, and can always find a few choice words (appropriate, of course) to say to them. I am not an angel, I am a teacher and an advocate.

Full of patience. I am patient, but no more patient than the average person. I don't mean to shock anyone with this confession, but I get frustrated like any other professional in any other job. I set goals and have expectations for my students, and when I know that they are able to meet them, but won't, I do get frustrated. I once had a stand-off with one of my students over signing the word shoes. All I wanted her to do was sign the word, and though she had signed it several times in the months that preceded this moment, she would not sign it for me. One simple request turned into a five-minute staring contest, and ended with me eventually helping her sign it just so that we could move onto the next activity. I was frustrated with her for not performing a simple task that I knew she could do, and I was frustrated with myself for making it such a big issue. As soon as the moment was over, it was like it hadn't happened. We continued on with our day in the usual way. I am not full of patience, I try to set realistic expectations for individual students based on their abilities.

Assumptions about my students

Helpless. In the six-plus years I have been at Beverley, I have never seen a helpless student. My students spend every minute of every day striving to meet goals set by themselves, their families, and their school teams. Each day, students in my class work on developing independence, whether it be standing for two seconds without assistance, or touching a switch attached to a toy in order to activate it. A student of mine started attending school without being able to hold a spoon independently, let alone bring it to his mouth. One day, after two and a half years of working on holding the spoon (my hand over his hand) and lifting the spoon (my hand over his hand), and bringing the spoon to his mouth (my hand over his hand) he was sitting in front of his lunch, reached out his hand, picked up his spoon, and brought it to his mouth. In those swift motions, he laughed in the face of helplessness (while we, the staff, all cried out of happiness!). My students are not helpless, they are determined and hard working.

Incapable of emotions. My students don't talk, that's true. They can't tell me that they are happy or sad, they can't tell me that they really enjoyed an activity, and they can't say how much they like me. They don't have the words, but they certainly have the emotions. My students speak with their smiles, frowns, grunts, laughter, eye movements, vocalizations, body movements, tears, and even their breathing.

I had a student who was learning how to walk, and part of her daily routine was to use parallel bars to walk about three meters independently. While I waited at the end of the parallel bars, she started walking towards me. As she got closer, she wanted to quit. She yelled at me with the sounds from her throat, she glared at me with her eyes, and she stomped her feet as she walked. She stopped a few times and bounced her body in anger. She was mad, but she didn't have to say a word to get her point across to me. Of course, though, I made her continue to walk until she reached the very end.

When she finally got to me, she wrapped her arms around me and collapsed into my arms, moved her head so she could lock eyes with me, smiled, tossed her head back, and laughed out loud. She didn't have to thank me for pushing her, and she didn't have to tell me she was proud of herself. Her body told me everything. My students are not incapable of emotions, they are bursting at the seams with them.

Can't learn. My students can't tell you what 2 + 2 is. They can't name the provinces in Canada. They can't write a proper sentence. But my students can learn. Every day they are faced with the challenge of learning—they are inundated with information: lights, sounds, words, faces, toys, smells, and textures. In class, I play the guitar and sing for my students as often as I can. I find music to be engaging, exciting and universal as both a teaching and a learning tool. One day I sang the name of one of my students. He looked straight at me and smiled. Well, I couldn't stop there. He acknowledged that I sang his name, so I wanted him to sing mine. So I continued throughout the weeks to sing his name with those same notes, and he continued to smile at me. Then he started to make noises deep in his throat in response to his name. Then he began to move his mouth while making those vocalizations. After a few months, I would sing his name, and he would mimic me and sing back to me. His responses demonstrated commitment in learning. He worked on developing the skills he needed to respond to me appropriately. It took a lot of hard work, a lot of repetition, and a lot of time, but he did it. This was five years ago, and when I see him in the hallways, I will approach him and sing his name. He looks at me, smiles, and sings right back to me. My students aren't unteachable; they are constantly learning.

Don't belong in school. This is probably the assumption that frustrates me the most. I do not work in a day care. I do not work in a group home. I am a teacher, and my job description matches that of teachers who work in grades kindergarten to eight in every school in Ontario. I teach my students skills that they need in order to function in their lives for the present time and the future. Regardless of what we are doing or where we are, we are engaged in educational moments and activities. A trip to The Grange (a local community building with ten to twenty food vendors inside) isn't just a walk, it's an experience. My students get a chance to smell foods from different areas of the world, have a chance to taste things they may never taste at home, and get a chance to hear languages spoken by people at the next table that they may have never heard before. They are exposed to both sensory and cultural experiences that help them to determine their likes and dislikes. It tests their ability to utilize the skills they already have in a novel environment. My students belong in school, and just like every other child in the world, deserve the right to an education.

When I started working at Beverley School, I was excited to be a teacher. I have since been honoured with the roles of advocate, entertainer, decipherer, singer and friend. My students have taught me as much as I have taught them. I work hard, but they work harder. They ask for respect and understanding, and in return perform tasks that have been asked of them. They are filled with determination and success. They are capable of creating and maintaining friendships and connections. If there is one thing I want my community and the strangers that we encounter to know, it is that myself and my students are blessed with rich and meaningful experiences every day. But if assumptions need to be made, please assume that we are all just human beings simply living our lives to the best of our abilities, just like everyone else.

Collaborative Project

BEVERLEY KIDS WILL TEACH YOU

BY REBECCA ANSLEY

as long as you don't give up, it doesn't matter how slowly you go

yesterday and tomorrow really don't signify

it's important to giggle

power struggles are futile

it's better to be barefoot whenever possible

it's not healthy to hold your feelings in

it can take a lot of effort to understand what other people feel, but it's usually worth it

be who you are

the optical illusion of a spiralling fan is really cool

it's okay to say "I'm not okay"

a sense of wonder is a wonderful thing

Group Project

ROOM 110

BY ROBERT BICKFORD

I flip through some books of fairy tales in the school library. The large sparkly cover of *Rapunzel* stands out. My students love things that sparkle and light up, and Rapunzel's hair reminds me of Madeleine's hair. She's eleven years old. Like many of the students at Beverley, Madeleine has a rare disorder. The education system calls Madeleine and my other students *Non-Verbal, Developmentally Delayed, Physically Disabled, Low-Incidence, Autistic* and *Globally Delayed*. Doctors have even more labels. I know them as Nathan, Melissa, Faizal, Edwin, Kieran, Kyle and Madeleine.

I pull *Rapunzel* off the shelf, leave the library and walk down the hallway toward my classroom. It's 10:52.

Memona, my student volunteer, stands in the hall outside the classroom door in between Faizal and a large planter with lush green ferns hanging over the side. Faizal, who's seven years old, stands on his tippy toes. His tendons have developed in a way that pulls his heels off the floor. He holds his arms out in front of him like divining rods that find trouble instead of water. He's trying to get around Memona so he can get a handful of ferns.

"Faizal, you can use your hands for playing." Memona takes hold of Faizal's hands and guides him toward an xylophone on a bench nearby.

For many years, when Faizal was integrated into a classroom of typically developing children, he spent most of the day in his wheelchair. Here at Beverley Public School, we give him as much time out of his wheelchair as possible. We offer him time and space to work on self-regulation, to build his range of movement, and, occasionally, to trip and fall and get back up again. He is working toward spending a whole school day without the use of his wheelchair. Memona and I watch Faizal concentrate on plinking just the right xylophone keys in the tune of something that sounds like the ABC song. He has a knack for mimicking beats and melodies.

"Memona, we'll have storytime in five minutes."

She glances at the book in my hand. "Sure, we'll come back in soon."

I nod, smile, turn and open the door to the classroom.

Edwin, who's twelve years old, slouches slowly to his knees beside the large blue table in the middle of the room. Swaran, one of the three educational assistants in my classroom, who has a teenage child with a developmental delay, sees Edwin, swoops down, grabs one of his arms, holds the back of his neck, and eases his shaking body to the floor. Edwin's mouth opens in pain. His head wrenches to the right side. His eyes twitch.

I toss the book onto the table and kneel down next to Edwin.

"I will hold him while you get the magnet," Swaran tells me.

I pull off the black magnet with a fluorescent pink sticker wrapped around Edwin's arm. I hover the magnet over the implant in his chest to activate the calming signal that rushes through his nervous system. Edwin's eyelids flutter.

"There you go Edwin, you're okay. You're okay. It's gonna be okay," I reassure him.

Swaran tucks a pillow under Edwin's head. His eyes seem vacant. His body shakes. Drool spills from the corner of his mouth, down the pillow, and onto the floor.

I hear screaming from the other end of the classroom.

"Swaran, can you stay with Edwin?" I ask. She nods.

"Edwin, you are alright. You will be alright," Swaran says.

Swaran's comforting voice fades as I step toward the screaming. I know it's Kieran. Kieran, who's ten years old, tantrums. If he doesn't feel like walking, he drops to the floor and screams. If another student starts lunch before him, Kieran moans and cries. If Kieran sees a new person in the room, he shrieks louder. When we go for walks or field trips, Kieran screams if he's too warm or he wants to be carried. Strangers look at us as if we're torturing him. Together with Kieran's parents, we have decided to ignore his tantrums and he's doing much better. He has only a couple brief meltdowns each week.

Janet is helping him to sit in preparation for storytime. He makes small panicked jumps in front of the chair where we are asking him to sit. Janet stands next to him and holds his left arm.

Kieran yanks, pinches and pulls at his forest green GAP sweater. Tears roll down his cheeks and mix with the drool and snot around his mouth. The shrieking pierces my ears. Janet speaks softly to him, "It's okay, Kieran. It's time to sit for story."

I walk to the counter, pull a few tissues from the box and bring them to Kieran's face. I try to wipe the tears and saliva and drool from around his nose as he jumps and shouts in short bursts. I throw the tissues away and wash my hands.

I walk back and sit next to Edwin on the floor. He looks up at me and grins. I place the palm of my hand on the side of his head. I look at him. He looks at me. "Hey Edwin, welcome back. You're alright buddy. It's good to see you."

Swaran pulls out one of the bright orange bean bag chairs for Edwin to rest on while we start storytime.

"Edwin, we're going to pick you up so you can rest on the bean bag chair," I tell him.

Swaran counts, "One, two, three."

We pick him up, place him in a sitting position and put a small, red plastic, electric guitar that plays "It's a small world afterall" when he pushes one of its yellow buttons, onto his lap. Edwin loves buttons. "There you go, Edwin. Enjoy," I tell him.

I look up at the clock. 10:58. I scan the classroom. Madeleine sits in a small, red chair near the window. Nathan, who's ten years old, sits at a wooden table against the wall. Holding a purple stacking cup in his mouth, he plays with a felted butterfly with shiny beads sewn into it. Beside Nathan, Melissa, who's eight years old, stands in a device that keeps her body in an upright position to build her leg and back strength. She has minimal use of her right arm and hand. Her swinging left hand makes up for it. She whooshes it down near Nathan's head and then pulls it up on the tray in front of her brushing over the colourful spinning mirror toy. She taps her sneakers, sways her head, and curls her arm as though she were a practising ballerina.

"Yes, yes, Kyle, you're doing it all on your own," Jian says. Jian stands beside Kyle ready to catch him if he sways back or forth. Kyle, who's thirteen years old, steadies himself with his arms in the air. With his long, curly brown hair, he looks like a surfer riding a wave for the first time. Kyle wears skull print wristbands and has a full drum kit at home. He'll soon be a big brother, a super cool one.

"Whoa, great job Kyle! Nice standing buddy," I tell him, as he concentrates with his eyes fixed on one spot. He swats away Jian's arms. One corner of his mouth curls up. He chuckles. He focuses on his balance. Kyle is working on increasing his independence skills. He enjoys the challenge of standing on his own.

"Jian, it's storytime so keep Kyle here and we'll bring everyone else over to make a circle," I say. "Yeah, yeah, sure, sure," Jian says.

I hear the door slam open. Bonk! I look back to the other end of the classroom and see the steel door bounce back slowly after hitting the white concrete wall. Faizal rolls into the classroom in his yellow wheeling walker that looks a bit like a bicycle with training wheels and no pedals. Faizal gives the door another forceful push and glides his walker into the room.

"You read my mind, Faizal! We're about to start our story," I call out. I look at my watch. 10:59.

Faizal peddles his legs along the floor, rolls past the washroom door and slides his small fingers around the edge of a Garfield poster that reads, "It's easier to get into things than out of them." He gets a hold of the poster's edge, pulls the corner of it off the wall, smiles, looks at me, and waits for my reaction. I have learned not to respond to these behaviours because when I do, the behaviour stays put.

Memona scurries around him, grabs the poster, and pats it back on the wall. "Hands to yourself, Faizal," Memona says, looks at me, and smiles.

"Okay everyone, can we please form our circle for storytime, over near the corner," I announce.

Swaran helps Melissa out of her standing device. She faces Melissa's back. She holds her arms above her elbows. They take baby steps together.

I help Nathan into a standing position. He still holds a purple stacking cup in his mouth and the felted butterfly in his hand. He reaches for my glasses to put them in his mouth too. "Hands to yourself, Nathan. Time for story," I say, hold his hand, keep him steady, and help him to his chair in the circle. Memona lifts Faizal out of his yellow walker and into his chair, ready for story.

I walk over to Madeleine who sits in a chair next to the window. She'll be unhappy with whatever change of position I ask her to make. Her digestion has caused her a lot of pain this morning. Her constipation sometimes lasts days.

"Madeleine, we're going to stand up and walk together to circle. You can sit down again but we need to get up and walk now."

She's tries out a few different chairs and rockers to ease the pain of the gas trapped in her body. She holds her thumb in her mouth and makes a spitting sound with her tongue. Other teachers have called this *making raspberries* on her report cards. I kneel down. She kicks one of her feet up at my shin. I smile. She kicks again.

I move closer to her face. Her brown eyes move slightly. She seems to be looking at me but I don't know how clear I come through. "Madeleine, it's time to stand up. Hand down from mouth, please," I whisper.

"Hand down from mouth, please," I repeat.

She doesn't move.

I tug lightly at her left hand clamped firmly in her mouth. She pulls her hand down out of her mouth and under my grasp. The saliva leaves a spot on her pants. The skin between her thumb and index finger is raw from making raspberries. She tightens her whole body. She grunts.

"Okay, on three Madeleine. One, two, three." I pull her to her feet. She grunts again and stiffens like a board. I stand behind her, holding her under her armpits. She brings her left hand back into her mouth. She shuffles a little. I nudge her legs and feet forward a couple inches at a time.

Faizal, Melissa, Kyle and Nathan sit ready for story. I get Madeleine to the front of her chair and ease her into a sitting position. She starts making raspberries again, spraying her soaked pink shirt. I look toward Swaran to ask her to get Madeleine a change of shirt, but Swaran has already headed to Madeleine's backpack to get one. I look at my watch. It's 11:03.

Memona takes *Rapunzel* from the blue table and hands it to me. I sit on a rolling stool in the middle of the circle, take a deep breath, and look around at Kyle, Nathan, Faizal, Madeleine and Melissa. Kieran and Edwin will join the circle when they are ready.

I show the cover of the book to Kyle. He looks at the image, then pats it like a drum. I show the cover to Nathan. He grabs the edge of the book and brings it toward his mouth. I bring the book to Madeleine and encourage her to pat the image of Rapunzel's shimmering hair. Swaran waits behind her with a dry shirt in her hand. Madeleine looks at the image and whacks the book away from her.

I open the book and begin. I show the picture to Faizal. He looks intently at the image and pulls the book from my hands and grins. I take the book back and show the image to Kyle and then to Melissa. She smiles and makes a high-pitched, happy sound and swings her left hand at the page.

Tile Project

YES AND NO

BY ROBERT BICKFORD

"We want to encourage her communication," Madeline's parents say. I shuffle in my chair, look down at the large blue table in front of us, then look up over Madeline's parents shoulders at a bulletin board covered in learning goals, for each of my seven students in Room 110 here at Beverley School in Toronto.

In bold black letters, Madeline's learning goal says "use a consistent communication strategy."

"So what ways is she communicating now?" I ask.

"In so many ways, she's so communicative!" Madeline's Mom interjects.

"Okay, in what ways is she most consistently communicating?" I ask.

"Well, she shakes her head for *No*, and sometimes nods for *Yes*. She also claps for *Yes* when we ask her questions," Mom tells me.

"So we can work on making that communication more clear to people who are new to Madeline. If you'd like, we can try attaching two switches to her tray. We'll start with one for *Yes* and ask her questions like, 'Do you need to go to the washroom' or 'Are you hungry' and see if she locates and figures out the meaning of the *Yes* switch. When she tries to clap for *Yes* we'll encourage her to use the red switch instead. Then, if we're seeing success, we could add a *No* switch. A yellow switch for *No*.

"Does that sound okay for the next month or two, and I'll keep track of how well she's using the switches?" I ask them.

Madeline's Mom and Dad agree that would be a good next step for Madeline, to see if she can connect meaning to the switches.

Madeline's Mom records her motherly voice saying *Yes*.

To the tray of Madeline's wheelchair, I attach a switch that plays the recorded *Yes* when pressed.

We encourage Madeline to use the switch. Her vision is strong enough that she can see the red switch on her tray. She uses it, sometimes. She answers questions, sometimes. When we start having more success, Madeline's parents ask to add the yellow *No* switch, and so we do.

Madeline doesn't show as much success making distinguishing between the red and yellow switches to answer questions.

Other staff at the school notice Madeline's switches on her tray. Since they've only seen Madeline communicate using gestures and body movements, and a few sounds for pleasure or discomfort, they are surprised to see a *Yes* and *No* switch on her tray. They are surprised when I tell them that Madeline can shake and nod her head to respond to questions, sometimes.

Sometimes, staff come up to Madeline and ask her a question to see if she will respond, to test out the switches themselves. Madeline has used them, sometimes.

I overhear other staff talk about Madeline's *Yes* and *No* switches. They wonder if she is using them. They wonder why we are trying out this system. They wonder if its too advanced for Madeline. At teacher staff meetings, there's discussion about whether communication strategies need to include *Yes* and *No*.

In the end, Madeline doesn't use the switches consistently and so we take them off. I am glad we tried to give Madeline a chance to say *Yes* and *No* more clearly. I know Madeline's Mom and Dad are glad we tried.

Kiyoshi

Room 117 Collaboration

BEVERLEY SCHOOL

BY SABRINA MOREY

Beverley is the only school I have ever worked at. And, I think that even if I searched my whole life, I would still end up here. I write this in the midst of feeling exhausted at the end of a really long day—the kids were particularly busy today, having been up a little later than usual at our school BBQ last night. My own one-year-old daughter came home from daycare with a burned hand yesterday; the blisters are big and ugly and make her generally cranky and irritable. But still, somehow my day job doesn't feel as much like a job as it does my regular life.

Isn't it normal to write home to parents about poo everyday? It doesn't strike me as unusual to phone someone up with a four-year-old on my lap and cheer about peeing on the potty! In fact, I have become accustomed to riding my bike home with a photograph of a toilet dangling from my waist. We potty train with pride. A stranger might judge me, but if you are part of the Beverley community, you'll understand.

I think being a part of this school, an extension of my family really, has taught me more than I could ever teach any student. I have learned about paying attention to details—searching for clues, evaluating patterns, and reading people closely to discover needs, likes and dislikes and new ways to see the world. I have learned how to have fun—whether it means playing with soap suds or jumping up and down repeatedly. Smiles at Beverley come easily. I have learned how to feel with others—the highs and lows and everything in between. Emotions are often close to the surface and working amongst such a supportive group allows me to process a wide range of emotions safely. And, perhaps most importantly, I am continuing to learn as I raise a new little person in my family and relate to all of this in a whole new way.

    Why would I spend my day anywhere else?

Tile Project

Classroom Collaboration

COMING OF AGE

BY SPENCER STANDISH

The moment in my life when I came of age was when my little brother John passed away. I was in grade seven. I remember the moment so clearly, all the horrible emotions I felt. What I remember most of all was walking into my living room where my brother had been sitting for days breathing and sleeping, except this time he wasn't breathing, sleeping, smiling or frowning; he was dead.

My little brother was ten years old.

John was born on March 9, 1998, and for all his life he had a disability. I remember my parents telling me when I was young that there was a virus in his brain that kept his brain from developing but his body would continue to grow like a normal young boy. I hadn't realized what this meant until my Johnny started growing up and hadn't spoken any words and hadn't begun walking at the average age most children do. Nonetheless, I loved my little brother with all my heart. I didn't care if he was disabled or couldn't speak. I knew he could hear what I was saying and I knew he loved me.

When I was going into grade seven, my Johnny was going into grade five, and around the start of the school year he started getting really sick. Since he was a baby, my parents and the doctors had been trying to figure out what was wrong with him and hopefully find a cure. No one knew. My parents had seen one of the greatest doctors in Canada in his field of expertise, because our main doctor in Toronto wanted a second opinion on what he thought the problem was. Sadly, the doctor in Ottawa was no help to us either, because he too couldn't understand what the problem was. Just after Labour Day in 2008, my parents realized that Johnny wasn't in good enough condition to go back to school. My family had just finished renovating the back of our house and there was this great big living room, so my parents brought down a bean bag bed from upstairs and sat Johnny down in it and this was where he spent most of his time until he passed away. My parents called a nurse and had one nurse on a full day shift to watch over him and a different nurse for the night shift. Johnny was on oxygen and his pulse was constantly checked. Sadly, my parents knew he was coming to the end of this life, and this news was very hard for me and my older sister Madeleine to hear.

I told myself that I would spend as much time with my little bro as possible, until the moment he dies. Johnny died on September 25th, 2008. The night before, on the 24th, I lay down beside him in his bean bag bed, just talking to him and telling him everything he meant to me, and I knew he was listening. I remember telling him that he didn't have to suffer anymore. I told him I loved him very much but I'd rather him be free and happy in heaven than in pain and immobile on earth, and so I told him he could go if he wanted. That night, on the 24th, I cried myself to sleep with my arms held tightly around him and my cheek resting on his face. On September 25th, at around 4:30 p.m., I remember my parent's friend Emily, who had been with us visiting, coming outside. She told us we should come inside. My heart skipped a beat. I ran inside as fast as I could, but when I arrived in the living room, it was too late; he was gone. It was the most horrible experience of my life; you haven't felt sorrow until you've lost your best friend and your brother in the same day.

I came of age at that moment. It is something I'm going to remember forever.

My little brother taught me how to be a better person. He taught me how to love and cherish the world without ever saying a word. He taught me to live everyday to the fullest because life's too short, and unfortunately, it was way too short for him. I love Johnny more than everything in the world and nothing is going to change that. John has made me caring and loving to many other disabled children and I don't believe I would be the same person I am today if John hadn't been my little brother. He has made me stronger, kinder, gentler and more loving, and I am forever grateful and proud to call John Standish my brother.

Group Project

THANK YOU FOR YOUR CHILDREN

BY STACIE CARROLL

Music blaring, we move the furniture aside and dance. We twirl and swing, laughing out loud. Arms raised and feet moving, wheels spinning, holding hands. Paint is splattered, sand tossed, blocks stacked and knocked to the ground while we cheer and clap.

Thank you for your children. Thank you for trusting me to care for them and teach them.

I don't presume to know or understand what life is like for you at home. I don't know the stress and worry that must reside within you and keep you up at night. I also don't know the joy and love that obviously fills your home, so clear and present in the faces of your children. What I do know is that your children are wonderful. I cherish every day I get to spend with them. I also think that the balance might be tipped in my favour; that I have learned more from you and your children than I feel I have taught.

There is a reason teachers and educational assistants talk about a class of students as being "ours." Our class, our students. Together, we take seriously the trust and responsibility you share with us in our positions. Your children become a part of our class and school family. We strive to make each day at school the best day ever for your child. We sing and dance and play and learn. We soak in each giggle, smile, choice made, and accomplishment. We celebrate everything. When someone gets hurt, has a seizure or gets sick, we worry and try to stay calm as we support them.

As a teacher, I have learned more about neurology, gastric procedures, anatomy, growth patterns and various drugs than I thought possible. I always remember that while this may be the 112th parent meeting I have had, it is your first. I may have known dozens of children who have been on this same drug, but none of them have been your child. I have helped students test and trial hundreds of walkers and standers, but never with your child.

There are images and experiences shared with your children that live with me every day. First steps, first words, clear choices, small successes that resonate with a sonic boom. I miss the children who have died. I can see each of their faces, remember their voices, and the feeling of their hand in mine.

I am changed because of you and your children. I hope I have become a better teacher, mother and person through each new experience.

Thank you for your children.

Tile Project

BLOWING BUBBLES

BY STELLA KYRIACOU

A rmya learned how to blow bubbles with me in the fall of 2012. We had been working on this skill for many weeks. I decided to start humming in the water and guide his hand over my mouth under the water to feel the vibrations and bubbles. He instantly loved it! He then copied me and started blowing bubbles! He and I were so happy.

SWIMMING

BY STELLA KYRIACOU

Soaib and I had been working on swimming in a horizontal position in the water. We tried a water belt instead of his regular water wings. The belt forced his body to be horizontal in the water and he just started to kick and move his arms and laugh with a huge smile on his face. It was the best moment!

Tennyson and Stephanie Quance. Photo by Michelle Quance

MY SISTER TENNY

BY STEPHANIE QUANCE

My name is Stephanie Quance. I am sixteen years old and have two younger siblings, Ethan who is fifteen, and Tennyson who is twelve. Tennyson is severely autistic. She cannot speak or communicate with us, but she brings joy to my family everyday. She is always smiling and laughing.

Even though Tenny needs help with almost everything, last year my mom came up with an idea to get Tenny involved in some things that I do. I am a competitive Irish dancer, and whenever I am practising, Tenny is always smiling and hopping along. When my dance school decided to host our own competition, we got the idea to enter Tenny into the Special Child competition. I was unsure at first, not knowing if Tenny would co-operate on stage or be in a good mood.

Before the competition my dance teachers held a mini practice, where we played some Irish dance music and Tenny jumped around. They even offered to let Tenny wear our school competition dress. Even though there was only one in Tenny's competition we did not care. It was just for fun and to make Tenny happy.

On the morning of the competition, we styled her hair and put her in the dance dress and shoes. When we were side stage, I told Tenny to just jump around, move a lot, and just don't stop. I wasn't sure she would understand. I was nervous that she was going to stand still, or worse, sit down! I then brought Tenny on stage and held her hand. Everyone was there to watch, all of my friends, family and dance teachers.

When the music began, Tenny immediately started hopping up and down and moving her feet. Everyone was clapping along to the music. Tenny had the biggest smile on her face. At the end of her dance, the judge came on stage and hugged her. It was one of the best memories. Everyone was so happy and amazed. It was just the best seeing Tenny perform and enjoying the day.

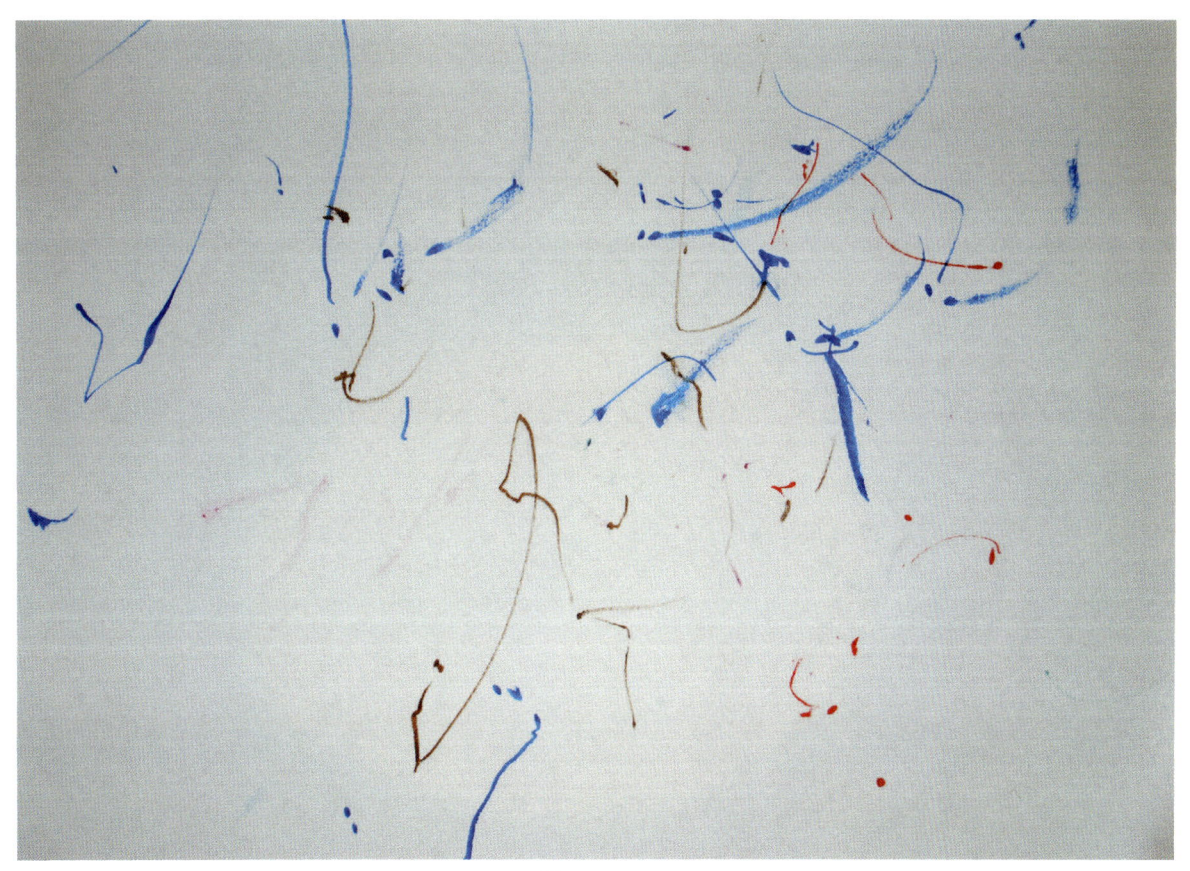

Tennyson

Classroom Project

THE STORY OF ZHELA LERWOB

BY STEPHEN SUEN

> *Before writing up the following story, I did fifteen minutes of free write, and from what I wrote, I picked up some key words such as autistic, shaking head and hands, screaming, groaning, whining, punching forehead, pinching, scratching, bite, strong grasp, reaching out, pulling, knock down furniture, mouthing hands, interacting with toys, books, soil, leaves, sand, and deep touch. And with these key words, I determined to write a short story about a child with this unique characterization. This child's name is Zhela Lerwob.*

Zhela and I have known each other for two years. Within these two years, we worked, played, danced, talked, read and shared our feelings together. I know him in a very profound way, but this story is about Zhela himself. I wish Zhela could write his story here, but he cannot write it because of his conditions. Zhela and I have built up a very trustful relationship and I am sure that he would not mind me pretending that I am him to write this story. Here is the story.

It begins with my name. Yes, yes, my name is Zhela Lerwob, a very special name because I am special as I was identified since I was twelve months old. My dad, somehow, was very angry for having me as his son; he blamed my mom for carrying bad genes; and he often said to my mom that it was too stressful to live with me in the same house. I have no memories about those days living with my dad, but what I can remember was one day my dad, without giving my mom any warning or notice, suddenly left us, and since the day he left, he never came back. So far, I am still not able to figure out what problems I cause to my family. What kind of problems could my family have because of me in it?

Anyway, I love my mom. Oh, yes, I love hugs from my mom. The tighter she hugs me, the better. Oh! I love it, and I love it dearly. Yes, like other children, I sleep when I am tired, but somehow in the morning when I get up, I feel a sense of loneliness in me. I look around, and seeing nobody around, I feel sad, and I weep, groan and cry in a low voice. Then, I feel pain in my head, particularly my forehead. This is excruciating pain. I punch my head with my fist, and somehow, it helps release my pain. I keep on punching my forehead, and I can't stop the excitement of doing it, and I groan, whine, shout and scream. If it so happens that an adult is beside me, I will grab their hand and bring it to my forehead—a gesture asking them to punch my forehead because I will feel good if they do it. I want the adult to punch harder, harder, but the adult is stupid because they either refuse to punch me or don't punch me hard enough. I get so angry and frustrated that I pinch, scratch and bite their hand. I even whine, shout and scream at the adult, but still the adult does not get my message. "Look, look how frustrated I am when dealing with these big people!"

I hate to look directly at a person's face. Why should I have to look directly at a person's face if I can see that person with my peripheral eyesight? Great! This year they do not expect me to do it.

I hate wearing my socks and shoes; I take them off soon after an adult puts them on me. I do not like wearing socks and shoes because they make my feet very uncomfortable. I take off my shoes as soon as I am on the school bus.

Then, I hate to see an adult coming onto the bus to pick me up and bring me into the school in the morning, because they always want me to put my socks and shoes on again. Not only that, the adult wants me to walk as well. Yes, I can walk for a short distance, but to be honest, I still enjoy being pushed around in my stroller rather than walking from place to place inside the school building.

Can any of the adults understand me at school!? No, no, no! Most of them don't!

Who can I trust?

Thank God. There are four people whom I trust dearly in the classroom. They are my teacher and three of his helpers.

Room 110

ONCE UPON A TIME

BY SUZANNE HEARN (PATERNAL GRANDMOTHER OF HAVANA)

Once upon a time there was a beautiful angel who lived up in heaven. In fact she was so beautiful and so loving that God decided that He wanted to share her with the people on earth who needed to be reminded of what true beauty is all about—not exterior beauty, but interior beauty that shines from the soul. He wanted her to be called Havana.

He explained to her what her mission on earth would be as well as the necessary conditions to accomplish this challenge.

He would have to give her a human body, temporarily. However, He would not give her the gift of speech or of independent mobility. Instead, she would be given very special needs, and a unique brain, which would require that she be totally dependent on her caregivers to meet all her basic needs. Otherwise, they could never learn from her what God wanted them to learn. They also had to be very special people.

He chose her parents very, very carefully. In fact, they were parents who believed that they would never be able to have any children together due to physical illnesses.

But God, in His wisdom, had a different plan when He sent her to them.

He gave them a hugely difficult and challenging twenty-four-hour-a-day task. Yet simultaneously He gave them the core strength of soul and spirit to carry out whatever Havana would need. He gave them the gifts of wise decision-making skills, unlimited dedication and unconditional love for their child. These traits enabled them to guide her and lead her into the hearts of the many, many people who are involved in her life. All have learned from her what love and gentleness of the spirit really is, in a few very short years.

Just imagine all the people whom she will touch while on earth!

Not only her parents, but her grandparents, her aunts and uncles, her entire extended family, her teachers, her physicians, her physical and occupational therapists, her schoolmates, her caregivers, her friends at church and in her neighbourhood. The list is endless! Havana will help all of us to become better individuals ourselves, just by being in her surroundings!

So many of us have learned to be more patient, more tolerant, more responsible and more appreciative of what we have because of her. We have learned new ways of communication without words by listening attentively to her sounds, by watching her expressions of interest, of sadness, of joy or pain. By experiencing the comfort she obtains just by being held in our arms and sung to. By including her in all our activities and outings. She has taught us so much more than she could have ever learned from us.

She brings out in us such intense degrees of acute awareness of love and tenderness—more than we could ever have imagined had she never touched us with her soul.

We love you Havana, and are so grateful that we have you in our midst. You fulfil even more than your mission in life simply by showing us, moment to moment in our daily lives, what true love and happiness is. You are so very special to all of us. We are so blessed and so happy to have you as part of our family.

Some day you will return to heaven. None of us know when that day will be, but we know that we cannot keep you with us forever; you have only been loaned to us. What a wonderful gift you have given, and continue to give us, every day! We do thank our God for His love and goodness in sharing you with us every single day of our lives.

Group Project

Student Group Project

MOTHERS OF BEVERLEY

BY TRACY PARSONS

Perhaps it's the fact that thirteen years ago I first walked through the doors of Beverley School as a woman very pregnant with my first child. Or maybe it's just because of the unique bond I see with mothers and their children. The first thing I think of when I think of Beverley School is the mothers. Sorry, all you dads. I see you. I see the work you put in, too. It's just that motherhood is my turf. It's what I know. My reference point.

As all women going through this journey can attest—motherhood—it's the one thing that can make you feel such utter joy and also such utter depletion, which brings me to the Mothers of Beverley Students. Don't mistake what I say for pity. I don't pity you. You have some of the most unique and amazing children that I have ever known. Parenthood is tiring, though.

Leaving Beverley School the end of some days, I didn't know where my energy was to come from for the next part of my day. Parenthood is busy, busy all the time. In those moments, I would think of you, Beverley Mothers. I would find strength from you, in knowing the journey you were on. I would think to myself, *Suck it up, Buttercup. These mothers are charting a new path. The one I'm on has been done for ages.*

You are pioneers. This is new ground.

So many mothers at Beverley School amaze me. One mother in particular had a huge impact on me. Your words on the bus coming home from the trip to Camp Cooch. Your raw and emotional praise of Beverley staff and calling us your family. I thought it so amazing that you were so open with us all. I felt so blessed to be on the bus that day and to hear your words.

That moment has had a lasting impact on me. I saw over those two days how ferociously you loved and fought for your son, how the journey to acceptance was still coming and how we get embarassed in public when our kids are "out of line."

I thought of that as I listened to your son ask loudly for McDonald's, at your funeral service. I wondered if you would have been embarassed. I wondered if you knew how much of an impact you had on so many of us at Beverley School. If you knew that you, Stella, made me want to be a better mother.

All mothers of students at Beverley School, I salute you. I thank you. Working with your children is something I will cherish forever. Even a year after I have moved on, I ache to see your children and to soak in the awesomeness that is Beverley School. May you all find peace on your journey. It's easy to question all of the choices we make for our children. This, I think, rings true for all mothers.

Classroom Project

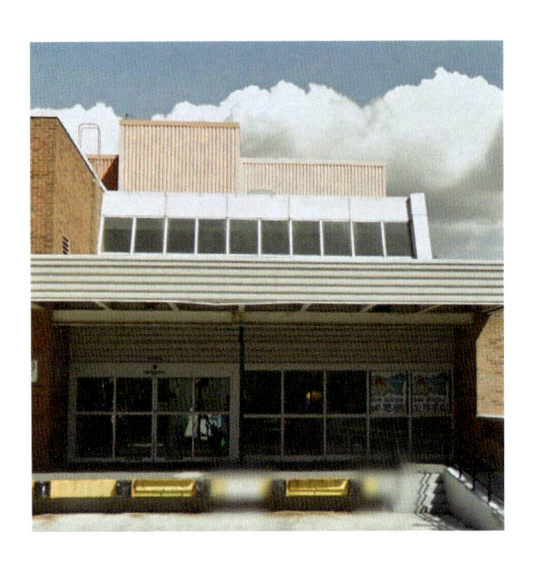

OH, BEVERLEY

BY ZOFIA CZERNIAWSKA

Oh Beverley, Oh Beverley
It's time for storytelling
The school where I work
It's unique…like New York!

Fifteen years have passed
And my work experience
and the Beverley School glow
Will last forever, I know!

My dear children
My beautiful souls
You're like the precious stones
And I love you all!

Alana, you're like our Mama
Oh Boy, did I say Mama?
My boss Alana!
Oh well, thanks for being a Mama
To all of us, Alana

Oh Boy, Oh Boy!
And that is not all
The lovely people I met
I remember you all

And you, my dear colleagues
Thanks for your help
Thanks for everything you do so well
Thanks for your smile
Thanks for everything
You rock, as well, so well!!!

Made in the USA
Charleston, SC
25 November 2013